MW00636404

FOLLOWING
THE
CALL

Insights for Those Entering the Ministry

JERRY T. HOLT

Palmetto Publishing Group
Charleston, SC

Following the Call
Copyright © 2020 by Jerry T. Holt

All rights reserved. No part of this publication may be reproduced, stored in a retrieval system, or transmitted in any form by any means, electronic, mechanical, photocopy, recording, or otherwise, without the prior permission of the publisher, except as provided for by USA copyright law.

Unless otherwise indicated, Scripture quotations are from the King James Version and the New King James Version of the Bible. All emphases in Scripture quotations have been added by the author.

Cover design by Palmetto Publishing
Edited by Patricia Bollmann

Printed in the United States of America

ISBN-13 978-1-64111-764-7
ISBN-10: 1-64111-764-8

Wise words from an esteemed elder; practical principles from a lifetime spent in ministry; helpful observations covering every age and stage of a minister's life. If you are serious about *Following the Call*, then this rich resource will be a blessing to you. I commend my friend, Pastor Jerry Holt, for a job well done!

Raymond Woodward — Executive Presbyter, United Pentecostal Church of Canada

—

The author brings a life of authentic ministry to this book, accented with stories, wit, applications, and wisdom for your benefit and pleasure. His writing style is personal yet poignant as he invites you into his study for a friendly but important conversation. Any young minister would be accelerated in his journey by spending time in this book with the author.

Stanley O. Gleason — Assistant General Superintendent, United Pentecostal Church International

—

This book is relevant, needed, and should be promoted inside and outside our fellowship. Thank you for the many hours you have taken to put your experience in writing. This has been like digging in a gold mine!

Gordon Mallory — International Missionary Evangelist

—

Having known the author and his family for over fifty years, it is a delight to have such wit and wisdom concerning the ministry in one handbook. After reading this, I found myself revisiting sections that spoke volumes of sound advice regarding the everyday dealings in a minister's life. While this book is intended for those entering the ministry, this volume would be a reminder and invaluable resource for seasoned ministers as well.

William J. Singleton – Former South Carolina District Superintendent

—

I enjoyed reading this book. I especially appreciated the chapter on "Taking Another Look at Success," which is an area many young men struggle with. Also, the section emphasizing we are not called to be editors of the Word is very needed. I look forward to obtaining a copy to share with my grandson.

Ronnie Mullings – Honorary General Board Member, United Pentecostal Church International

DEDICATION

To Fayetta, my beloved wife and companion on this journey for the past fifty-two years. Your godly example and prayers have been a source of strength and encouragement to me as we continue to *follow the call* of God together. Without your help this book would not have been possible.

CONTENTS

INTRODUCTION

"Old men for counsel; young men for war."

I was only nineteen when I received a letter from the draft board ordering me to report for induction into the US Army. It was the Vietnam War era, which meant many of the inductees would be sent there after basic training. Our instructors and drill sergeants were combat veterans, and their advice and training were intended to help us survive on the battlefield in a war-torn country. Tragically, over 58,000 young warriors did not survive. Their names are engraved on the Vietnam Memorial Wall in Washington, DC.

Statistics show that a portion of all who start out in the ministry will not survive. Some drop out due to burnout or the unrealistic expectations and demands placed upon them either by themselves or by others. Some fall prey to moral failure. Pressure on a minister's family can be overwhelming at times and may cause him or her to seek another profession. Financial struggles, spiritual battles, and church or marital conflicts can contribute to the decision to leave the ministry.

Following the Call explores some of the challenges inherent in the ministry and more important, offers strategies to avoid becoming a casualty so you can join Paul in saying,

> *I have fought a good fight, I have finished my course, I have kept the faith: henceforth there is laid up for me a crown of righteousness, which the Lord, the righteous judge, shall give me at that day: and not to me only, but unto all them that love his appearing. (II Timothy 4:7–8)*

I know what it is to struggle with the call of God; it made me fearful and aware of my own inadequacies, yet more afraid not to answer the call to ministry. Having graduated from Bible college with appreciation for all that was taught, there still hadn't been enough time to cover the many aspects of ministry and dealing with people I would need later.

Fortunately, I had a few mentors during my early years. One of them pastored in a neighboring city, and whenever I had a problem or needed someone to talk to, he would invite me over for coffee or lunch. While I listened, he would share with me the things he had learned from his years as a veteran pastor. I will be forever indebted to him for his kindness and for taking the time to invest in me.

Much like basic training instructors share their knowledge and survival skills with young recruits, it is my desire to simply share some things I have learned and observed from more than fifty years in the ministry, things I wish I had known when I first started out. Over time, I have read and gathered material from many sources, some of which I have forgotten. However, I have tried to acknowledge and give credit where it is due.

So, pull up a chair, my friend. Together let's examine a few lessons worth learning so that you too can successfully follow your call and finish well.

–JTH

Chapter One

THE CALL OF GOD

For ye see your calling, brethren, how that not many wise men after the flesh, not many mighty, not many noble, are called: but God hath chosen the foolish things of the world to confound the wise; and God hath chosen the weak things of the world to confound the things which are mighty; and base things of the world, and things which are despised, hath God chosen, yea, and things which are not, to bring to nought things that are: that no flesh should glory in his presence. (I Corinthians 1:26—29)

You might think God would choose the most skilled, qualified, talented, spiritual individuals for His work and service. But as we look through the biblical record, we discover that God most often chooses the flawed, the broken, the unlikely, the sin-stained and messed-up lives of men and women to fulfill His divine plan and purpose.

God does not depend on these people's abilities or talents. After all, He can bring water out of a rock, make a donkey speak, and cause a rooster to give an altar call. It is God's power and grace alone working through flawed lives to accomplish His plans, all for one reason: "That no flesh should glory in his presence."

---

*God does not call the qualified, but over time,
He qualifies those whom He calls.*

When God places His call upon an individual's life, He already knows what they have and don't have going for them. I have observed in others and learned through personal experience that the Lord never calls people to tasks they can accomplish without Him. That is why I say emphatically, "God does not call the qualified, but over time, He qualifies those whom He calls." This is an invaluable lesson to learn, one that may take time and repeated lessons before it sinks down into our understanding, yet it is absolutely essential to grasp. Read on to see how one of God's great heroes learned this lesson early in his ministry.

"Who am I?" Moses asked when God called to him from the burning bush to return to Egypt and lead the Israelites into the Promised Land. Moses protested because he knew he could not do it; in his own sight he was woefully inadequate. For one thing, he lacked speaking ability (sometimes called "pulpit presence" or oratory skill). Besides, his reputation was such that even if he did go back, neither the Egyptians nor the Hebrews would believe him or listen to him. Sure, he had received the best of everything Egypt had to offer, including a royal upbringing, a comprehensive education, and probably training to fill a high governmental position. Yet all of that had in no way changed his meek and introverted nature. It was ludicrous to think God would call a man so easily intimidated to wrest several million slaves from bondage to the most powerful country on earth. Surely the Lord had chosen the wrong man for the job!

God already knew all of these things about Moses. He also knew Moses needed to be brought to the realization that the task *could* and *would* be accomplished—based not on Moses' capabilities but on God's. God had designed every detail of His plan before He ever called Moses. All Moses would have to do was keep an ear tuned to God's directions and then follow through.

Moses was not the only one who struggled with feelings of inadequacy. The book of Judges records the shocked reaction of Gideon when an angel appeared to him and announced, "The Lord is with you, you mighty man of valor!" (Judges 6:12). Gideon quickly informed the angelic visitor he was anything but a mighty man of valor. In fact, Gideon came from the smallest tribe in Israel, his family was the least in that tribe, and (in his own eyes) he was the least of everyone in his family. After many confirmations and assurances from the Lord, Gideon saw a great victory over the Midianites. He realized that God was the one who won that victory; all Gideon had to do was follow God's instructions.

I think I can safely say that everyone who has heard the call of God into any area of ministry has felt inadequate and unqualified. We need to grasp the important concept that God is not concerned so much with our abilities as He is with our willingness to hear His call and respond to it. Rather than natural ability, the thing that impresses Him is an attitude of total dependency upon Him and His abilities.

The call to the ministry is a call to dependency.

In the Gospel of John, Jesus and His disciples had crossed the Sea of Galilee and were resting on a mountainside, possibly hoping for some downtime. It wasn't long before they looked up and saw a "great multitude" approaching because the people had seen "His signs which He performed on those who were diseased" (John 6:2). Jesus turned to Philip and asked him a question he clearly wasn't prepared to answer: "Where shall we buy bread that these might eat?" Verse 6 reveals that Jesus was testing Philip, "for He Himself knew what He would do." Philip responded in the same way most of us would—by trying to figure out how in the world he was going to feed the multitude. He knew his resources were inadequate; it would take over half a year's wages to buy enough bread for each one to have a bite. Andrew expressed a glimmer of faith when he said, "There is a lad here with five barley loaves and two small fish." Even as the words came out of his mouth, he realized the suggestion was ridiculous, for he asked, "What is that among so many?"

Jesus told the disciples to have the multitude (about five thousand men plus women and children) to sit in groups of fifty. He blessed the bread and fish, then gave the food to the disciples, who in turn distributed the loaves and fish to the crowd. When everyone had eaten their fill, Jesus commanded the disciples to gather up the fragments. What started out as only five loaves and two small fish ended up as twelve heaping baskets of leftovers!

The disciples had mistakenly thought they were called to *produce* the miracle that was needed instead of trusting in the divine miracle producer. They were simply to be the *distributors* of the miracle.

The disciples were reminded of this on more than one occasion. At the wedding at Cana when Jesus instructed the servants to fill the pots with water and serve the wine, He did what they could not do—turned the water into wine! On another occasion, after a futile night of fishing with no results, Jesus told the disciples to let down their nets one more time in the same place where they had caught nothing. At His word they threw out the nets and gathered them back in, bulging with squirming fish!

Standing at the tomb of their brother Lazarus, Mary and Martha felt helpless in the face of death and sorrow until Jesus asked that the stone be rolled away. Martha protested, "Lord, by now he stinks. He's been dead for four days." Jesus merely wanted them to exercise their faith by having the stone removed, and then watch Him perform the miracle.

We can fill water pitchers, let down nets, and roll away stones, but He is the One who does the miraculous. We are only the conduit, the vessel, the distributor of what He alone can produce. We are called simply to be obedient and totally dependent upon Him for everything.

Jesus set forth the first principle of the kingdom of heaven in the Sermon on the Mount when He said, "Blessed are the poor in spirit, for theirs is the kingdom of heaven" (Matthew 5:3). The word translated *poor* is from a Greek word meaning "to crouch or cower like a beggar, to be deeply destitute, or completely lacking resources." Jesus was not advocating material poverty as a good thing; rather, in the spiritual kingdom of God, those who recognize their spiritual poverty are blessed because all of heaven's resources are made available to them.

I was on my way to a Bible study, walking along a busy over-pass above a crowded, noisy street in Guangzhou, China, when I noticed her. She was sitting on the roadside dressed in ragged clothes. A lock of hair was stuck to the side of her sweaty face, and in her arms was a tiny child. She was a beggar, a familiar sight in those days. There was no government funding available, no food stamps, no low-cost housing to provide for her or her baby. She lived by begging, depending on those with more resources than she had to get through each day. I reached into my pocket and gave her the money I had with me. Her anxious face brightened with a weak smile of gratitude as she said in her dialect, "Thank you."

This woman was depending on someone with more resources than she had. Jesus taught, "Blessed are the poor in spirit." Those who are destitute and dependent, those with no other resources, are blessed, for all of heaven's resources are theirs for the asking.

This is the attitude we must have. We are destitute of the spiritual resources needed to carry out the work and will of God, but we have this promise: beggars have access to all the resources of the kingdom of heaven! The Lord invites us to bring our needs, our requests, and every challenge and situation to Him. He has an abundant supply of everything we lack.

And my God shall supply all your need according to His riches in glory by Christ Jesus. (Philippians 4:19)

He has and is everything we need. Whatever our situation may be at the moment, God already knows and is prepared for it.

Before Abraham arrived at the top of Mount Moriah, the Lord had a ram waiting in the thicket to be the sacrifice. Before Moses arrived at the bitter waters of Marah, there already was a tree growing nearby, ready to be cast in to make the bitter waters sweet. God has already provided for us everything we will need before we arrive on the scene. Our circumstance allows God to show His power and provision on our behalf for His glory.

Remember we are like beggars without resources, but the One to whom we pray has all the resources we will ever need. He is willing and ready to supply our needs! The psalmist underscored this when he wrote, "You open Your hand and satisfy the desire of every living thing" (Psalm 145:16). Where the finger of God directs, the hand of God will supply.

We must realize our call into the ministry was never based upon our abilities or talents, for we are totally dependent upon the Lord for everything we lack. Then we will find ourselves able to *follow the call*. Let's look at another important principle: the call is a call to obedience.

The call of God is a call to obedience.

The Bible contains several accounts of men who started out well, but hard times and poor choices caused them to end up as casualties. What can we learn from their examples?

Saul was literally head and shoulders above the men of his day. In the beginning, he was quiet, unassuming, even shy. In fact, when he was chosen to be the first king of Israel, he ran and hid from the crowd and had to be brought out to accept his coronation.

However, somewhere along the way, his kingly position clouded his thinking, and he forgot the One on whom he should be depending. He became more concerned with his public image and what people thought about him rather than what God thought about him.

The story unfolds in I Samuel 13. The prophet Samuel had told Saul to wait seven days for him in Gilgal before engaging the Philistines in battle. Samuel had promised that when he arrived, he would offer a burnt offering and peace offerings to the Lord. When the seventh day came with no sign of Samuel, Saul felt pressure closing in on all sides. Samuel had told him to wait, but war with the Philistines was imminent; for days they had been rallying at Michmash. Saul's men, overcome with impatience and fear, were beginning to scatter. Saul decided to take matters into his own hands and offered the sacrifice that only the man of God was qualified to offer. The smoke was still rising from the burnt offering when Samuel arrived.

> Samuel said, "What have you done?" Saul said, "When I saw that the people were scattered from me, and that you did not come within the days appointed, and that the Philistines gathered together at Michmash, then I said, 'The Philistines will now come down on me at Gilgal, and I have not made supplication to the LORD.' Therefore I felt compelled, and offered a burnt offering." And Samuel said to Saul, "You have done foolishly. You have not kept the commandment of the LORD your God, which He commanded you. For now the LORD would have established your kingdom over Israel forever. But now your kingdom shall not continue. The LORD has sought for Himself a man after His own heart, and the LORD has commanded him to be commander over His people, because you have not kept what the LORD commanded you. (I Samuel 13:11–14)

Waiting is never easy. The urgent things in life always seem to crowd out the important things. Someone said, "If God is with you, why hurry? And if God is not with you, why hurry?" Good advice. The important thing we must remember is to remain obedient and trust in God's timing under pressure. When we get impatient and take matters into our own hands, we usually will regret it later.

Saul forgot the call to be king was God's idea, not his own. Whatever God starts He is capable and prepared to finish if we will learn to trust and obey His instructions. Saul's final downfall came when Samuel told him to avenge Israel against the Amalekites and not spare anything that had to do with them. "Saul attacked the Amalekites from Havilah all the way to Shur, which is east of Egypt" (I Samuel 15:9). But rather than obeying God's command to utterly destroy the Amalekites and everything they had, Saul spared their king and "all that was good," including the best of the sheep, oxen, fatlings, and lambs. "But everything despised and worthless . . . they utterly destroyed" (I Samuel 15:9).

The Lord told Samuel of Saul's disobedience, and the next morning he began searching for Saul, finally finding him back at Gilgal. He asked Saul, "What then is this bleating of the sheep in my ears, and the lowing of the oxen which I hear?" Saul's excuse was the people wanted to keep the best for offering sacrifices to the Lord. Samuel replied, "Behold, to obey is better than sacrifice, and to hearken than the fat of rams. For rebellion is as the sin of witchcraft, and stubbornness is as iniquity and idolatry. Because thou hast rejected the word of the LORD, he hath also rejected thee from being king" (I Samuel 15:23). Too late, Saul learned that partial obedience is still disobedience.

*Too late, Saul learned that
partial obedience is still disobedience.*

God did not call us to be editors of His Word. It is not our place to pick and choose the commandments we will keep, which ones might be popular, and which ones we can ignore. Partial obedience is still disobedience. God has called us to total obedience regardless of the pressure, opinions, or agendas of others.

"The fear of man brings a snare, but whoever trusts in the LORD will be kept safe"

(Proverbs 29:25). This pressure becomes very real when people threaten to withdraw their financial support or leave the church or try to force you out unless you meet their demands.

However, pressure from people on the minister is not a new problem. Paul addressed the following words to Timothy:

> *Preach the word; be instant in season, out of season; reprove, rebuke, exhort with all longsuffering and doctrine. For the time will come when they will not endure sound doctrine; but after their own lusts shall they heap to themselves teachers, having itching ears; and they shall turn away their ears from the truth, and shall be turned unto fables. (II Timothy 4:2–4)*

This is where the rubber meets the road. If you are in God's will, trying to keep your spirit and doctrine right, God will keep you in His care. He is the One who has called you into His service. If you allow the pressure of people to dictate who you are and what you preach or stand for, you will become a hireling and not a shepherd. If you are depending on people for your income and security, your dependency is in the wrong place. You will feel the pressure and temptation to compromise to avoid dealing with the problem.

Don't ever fear people more than you fear God. Don't ever be more concerned about your image and position than your relationship with Jesus Christ. If you keep this in mind, you can avoid becoming a casualty.

Following the Call involves understanding God's ministers are not chosen for their talents or abilities. Jesus said, "Without Me you can do nothing." When ministers *remain* totally dependent upon the Lord for *everything*, they will have all the resources they will ever need to fulfill His plan and purpose for their lives. They can be certain pressure will come, but so will God's supply. "My God shall supply all your need according to his riches in Christ Jesus" (Philippians 4:19).

In the next chapter we will take a closer look at a few potential pitfalls you must be aware of in order to avoid becoming a casualty.

Chapter Two

TAKE HEED TO YOURSELF

Let him who thinks he stands take heed lest he fall
(I Corinthians 10:12).

It is a great honor to be called to preach the Word of God. To minister with God's anointing and power working through a frail human vessel and seeing lives changed by His power is truly an amazing privilege. Yet it is important that we watch our own steps, for we are not exempt from the dangers and pitfalls we are warning others to avoid. The apostle Paul said it this way: "Therefore let him who thinks he stands take heed lest he fall" (I Corinthians 10:12), and it is echoed in the biblical paraphrase by Eugene Peterson: "Don't be so naive and self-confident. You're not exempt. You could fall flat on your face as easily as anyone else. Forget about self-confidence; it's useless. Cultivate God-confidence" (I Corinthians 10:12, MSG).

For a thousand years the "Pioneer Cabin Tree" grew tall and majestic in a place that one day would be called California. In

1881, a hole was carved into the tree's 32-foot diameter trunk, big enough for about fifteen to twenty people to stand in. Still later, automobiles would drive through the opening. Each year thousands of tourists visited Calaveras Big Trees State Park to admire this magnificent tree that towered high into the sky. But on January 8, 2017, a massive storm toppled the giant sequoia, and it crashed to the ground, splintering into thousands of pieces. When the tree was examined, it was discovered that it had been dying for a long time. There was only one branch alive at the very top. The storm revealed the true condition of the tree.

How can a minister avoid the pitfalls, the unseen decay and death that may end with the same crashing ruin that brought down the Pioneer Cabin Tree? The Scripture repeatedly reminds us to take heed and keep watch over our own selves.

I keep under my body, and bring it into subjection: lest that by any means, when I have preached to others, I myself should be a castaway. (I Corinthians 9:27)

Take heed therefore unto yourselves, and to all the flock, over the which the Holy Ghost hath made you overseers, to feed the church of God, which he hath purchased with his own blood. (Acts 20:28)

Let's look at some of the pitfalls and perils those in the ministry must take care to avoid:

1. *The Barrenness of Busyness:* "They made me the keeper of the vineyards, but my own vineyard have I not kept" (Song of Solomon

1:6). These words of Solomon paint a picture of one who was busy taking care of the vineyards of others to the neglect of his own. This is a common pit any minister can easily fall into.

The demands upon a minister can be emotionally and physically overwhelming at times. Counseling individuals and families who are in crisis may be necessary at any hour of the day or night. There is the administration of the church and departmental meetings to plan for and attend. There is the constant dealing with finances or the lack thereof. Time is needed in the preparation of sermons and Bible studies week after week. There will be weddings and funerals and hospital calls to make. At times everything seems to come at a pastor all at once, not to mention the needs of the minister's own family. All of this along with taking care of his own home and business affairs is more than one person can manage in their own strength.

It is easy to become so busy in the work of the Lord that we neglect the Lord of the work.

The barrenness of busyness is a very real threat to our personal spiritual survival. It is easy to justify our lack of spending quality time tending to our own soul and relationship with the Lord. After all, we are busy taking care of the work of the Lord and His people, aren't we? No wonder we have so little time left to spend with the Lord of the work. We allow this to our own peril.

The Pioneer Cabin Tree kept standing long after it was dead—that is, until a violent storm toppled it. Likewise, ministers may seem to get by for a season of neglecting their relationship with the Lord, but if it is not corrected quickly, it is only a matter of time until the deadness within results in another tragic fall.

Martin Luther said, "I have so much business I cannot get on without spending three hours in prayer." When we are too busy to pray, we are too busy. We must stay connected to the source of our power and anointing if we are going to stay spiritually alive and effective. We must not allow ministry to keep us from Jesus! We must be on guard, calling ourselves into account. We must keep our own vineyard in good repair while we are trying to help others.

2. *The Pitfall of Pride*: "Pride goes before destruction, and a haughty spirit before a fall" (Proverbs 16:18). Pride was the downfall of Lucifer. He became filled with his own self-importance and thought the glory that was given to him was of his own creation. "God resists the proud but gives grace to the humble." (I Peter 5:5) Lucifer was cast out of heaven and stripped of his position. He operates now only by the permission of God for a short while longer.

Pride can take many forms, but at its core is the sin of self—exalting in our abilities, our talents, or our motives rather than being totally dependent upon God. Whenever we think our position or title gives us special exemptions, we are setting ourselves up for a fall. If we think that since we are in charge, we are right and no one can tell us any different, we are on a slippery slope. If we do not humble ourselves, we soon will be humiliated. Peter had a revelation of who Jesus Christ was, but then his next words brought a rebuke from Jesus, who said, "Get behind Me, Satan!" (See Matthew 16:16–23.) We may be called of God and minister with anointing, but that doesn't make us infallible. Peter learned that lesson the hard way.

King David had Nathan the prophet to hold him accountable for his actions. Solomon, on the other hand, had no one he would listen to. After all, who was going to counsel the wisest man in the world? As a result, he drifted far from the very God who called him to be king and blessed him with everything he had.

I have watched good men go from being humble and grateful for having been called to serve the Lord to becoming arrogant and self-willed, destroying everything God allowed them to have. Pride has the letter I in the middle—and so does the word sin. Pride is at the root of all other sins. It puts *I will* above *God's will.* All we have and are able to do is through God's grace alone. We cannot and we must not take any credit or boast of our accomplishments. Jesus said, "Without Me you can do nothing" (John 15:5).

3. Bitterness: "[Beware] lest any root of bitterness springing up cause trouble, and by this many become defiled" (Hebrews 12:15). Church members aren't the only ones who have to deal with abuse, mistreatment, and betrayal. You too will have opportunity to become bitter over the words and actions of others. Be aware that bitterness is a poison that, if you succumb to it, will kill you. There's no getting around it; we live in a flawed and sinful world. Offenses will come—and sometimes we may be the offenders.

Bitterness grows like a root when it is watered and kept alive. Whatever wrong or injustice you may feel you have suffered does not justify you to harbor bitterness and resentment in your heart. You have heard it said, "Two wrongs don't make a right." If we preach the mercy and forgiveness of God for things that seem unforgivable, we will have to practice what we preach in order to *follow the call.*

I have never been around people who were bitter without knowing they were bitter. Bitterness not only poisons the people who allow it into their spirit, but they tend to spread the poison, which in turn contaminates and defiles others. (See Hebrews 12:15.) Be careful that you don't pick up someone else's offense, because the poison will contaminate you. Remember you are hearing only one side of the story.

John Bevere wrote an excellent book, *The Bait of Satan*, which deals with offenses and forgiveness. It is a must-read for everyone—because everyone will at some point find themselves dealing with offenses and guarding against bitterness.

4 Envy and Jealousy: "For where envying and strife is, there is confusion and every evil work" (James 3:16). It is much easier to weep with those who are weeping than to rejoice with those who are rejoicing, while they are enjoying the good favor and blessing from God and you are going through difficult times. The devil will plant all kinds of poisonous seeds in your mind: *They don't deserve that good fortune. I have worked just as hard if not harder than they have. Why would God bless them and not me with an influx of new saints, a new building, or a financial windfall?*

When Joseph was lied on and thrown in prison, his fellow inmates might have felt sorry for him. However, when he was riding around in Pharaoh's chariot and overseeing everything in Egypt, they might have thought differently. You may see the rewards of faithfulness, but you don't know the sacrifice or the price paid by that man or woman of God to receive those rewards. It is important to realize envy and jealousy are really directed at God, who has allowed others to have things you might not have. Be careful of that green-eyed monster called jealousy. It will blind you to the many blessings you already have and rob you of your joy and relationship with the Lord.

Genesis 43:34 records how Joseph tested his brothers when he gave Benjamin five times more than they had been given. He recalled how jealous his brothers had been over his coat of many colors—so jealous of their father's favor that they had sold Joseph into slavery. When he saw they no longer were jealous and how they pleaded for their brother's release when the gold cup was found in Benjamin's sack, Joseph revealed himself to them. We must consider how God is observing our words and attitude when another minister is being blessed and we feel we are not. If we can rejoice with those that rejoice, the Lord will surely reveal Himself in our midst.

We seldom compare ourselves with those who have less than we do or who would be grateful to enjoy the things we often take for granted. Take heed and guard your steps from the snare of envy and jealously.

5. Moral Failure: "Whoever commits adultery with a woman lacks understanding; he who does so destroys his own soul. Wounds and dishonor he will get, and his reproach will not be wiped away" (Proverbs 6:32–33).

My wife and I were getting ready to turn in for the night when the phone rang. A distraught minister's wife was on the other end. Sobbing, she told of her husband admitting to being involved with a woman in the church. They wanted us to come to their home. When we arrived, it was very late, and we spent most of the night with them. The atmosphere was worse than mourning over a death, for in reality something had died that could never be resurrected. The man's family, his ministry, and the church he pastored all suffered damage and reproach.

Know that you are not exempt from this treacherous sin that has cast down many mighty men before you. If there ever was an area in your life where the verse "Give no place to the devil" applies, it is in this area. Our society is saturated with sexual promiscuity. With one click, the internet, cell phones, and computers can open up a Pandora's Box of evil.

Nelson Mandela asserted, "Marriage is not a cure for lust. If it were, then adultery would not exist. Self-control is still a requirement. Lust doesn't care if you are married or single. You may be Solomon in wisdom or David in praise or Abraham in faith or Joshua in war. But if you are not Joseph in discipline, you will end up like Samson in destruction."

I've never known people who have been tempted in this area and not recognized it as a temptation. They have to lie to themselves before they can lie to anyone else. Surely, they can see red flags waving, but they ignore them and cross the line to commit sexual sins. A minister must realize he is in just as much jeopardy from this trap as anyone else.

The Scripture declares, *"Flee fornication."* Your thoughts are either your best friends or worst enemies. Keep your thoughts and imagination under control of the Spirit of God. Find someone you can confide in if you are struggling in this area. The sin that will bring you down is the sin you try to hide and are afraid to deal with. Get help before it is too late!

I have talked to several men who fell under the spell of this devastating sin. They have told me they would give anything to have a chance to go back and undo the damage they have caused, but that is impossible. How much better it is for one to do everything he or she can to *avoid* falling into adultery and having to live with a load of regret.

Your status as a preacher doesn't exempt you from this sin. In fact, the devil delights in bringing a reproach on the ministry and the church of Jesus Christ through the moral failure of preachers. All ministers suffer when a fellow minister falls. Not only does it bring a reproach that time will not erase, but it causes people to question the integrity of every other minister they know. If a man would think of the consequences of entertaining the spirit of lust and adultery, he would never find it appealing. It destroys families, the children and spouses of those involved are damaged, and the church family is brought into reproach.

Moral failure destroys faith among those who are struggling to live for God in a wicked world. They ask themselves, "If the minister can preach and teach the Word of God and still fall into adultery, what chance have I to live above sin?" Adultery in the church is spiritual incest, for you are committing adultery with your sister in the Lord.

Don't open the door to this temptation. *Give no place to the devil!* Never counsel a person of the opposite sex alone; avoid being alone in the church or your office or anywhere else with a person of the opposite sex. Even if your actions are innocent, you could be accused of misconduct and your name and reputation could be ruined because of carelessness. Joseph fled the house where Potiphar's wife had found him alone. He was innocent, but there was no one to verify his story. Do everything you can to protect your reputation. In today's society the mere accusation of mis-conduct is enough to ruin a man and his ministry.

Your wife is your best guard against women with ulterior motives and seducing spirits. Your best defense against moral failure is to keep your own marriage in good repair. Don't be so busy helping others that you neglect your relationship with your own wife and family.

6. *Compromise*: The desire to attract a bigger crowd can cause a man to wonder about the credibility of the things he once believed. The popular *accommodating gospel* that is preached seeks to find the interests of today's secular-minded people and give them what they want to hear. Topics like "how you can prosper" and "how you can reach your full potential" appeal to the carnal mind and desires. Services that consist of a few skits and upbeat songs and a short inspirational message may leave everyone feeling good, but no one is really challenged or changed. It would seem that it doesn't matter how you live or behave through the week as long as you believe. The question is, "Believe what?" James tells us even the devils tremble because they believe there is one God. But a belief that does not call for a radical, positive change in one's behavior—whether in or out of the church—will not make disciples.

This accommodating gospel makes little of the cross and discipleship and presents a God whose main concern is your happiness and material prosperity. Adherents to this "gospel" say that sacrifice, commitment, separation from sin, and living a life for the glory of God no matter the cost, does not appeal and may offend people.

Dietrich Bonhoeffer states this plainly in his book, *The Cost of Discipleship*: "When Christ calls a man, he bids him to come and die." We are called to preach the gospel of the Lord Jesus Christ and to represent Him as He is, not as some would like Him to be. Matthew 5:15 (NLT) says, "No one lights a lamp and then puts it under a basket. Instead, a lamp is placed on a stand, where it gives light to everyone in the house."

Do we think the light of the gospel and the call to discipleship is too bright a light for some and needs to be put under a bushel basket? The Scriptures teach, "He who wins souls is wise" (Proverbs 11:30) and "to [speak] the truth in love" (Ephesians 4:15). There is no excuse for harshness and offensive conduct in presenting the gospel and the Word of God. We cannot however, apologize for the claims of the gospel nor for the demands of discipleship for fear people will go elsewhere. This pressure is real but certainly not new to our generation alone. Paul wrote the following to a young minister in the first-century church:

> *Preach the Word; be prepared in season and out of season; correct, rebuke and encourage—with great patience and careful instruction. For the time will come when men will not put up with sound doctrine. Instead, to suit their own desires, they will gather around them a great number of teachers to say what their itching ears want to hear. They will turn their ears away from the truth and turn aside to myths. (II Timothy 4:2–4, NIV)*

Crowds followed Jesus as long as He offered loaves and fishes, but when He issued a call to commitment, many of them turned away. Jesus even asked His own disciples, "Do you want to go away as well?" Peter replied, "Lord, to whom shall we go? You have the words of eternal life." (See John 6:66–68, ESV.)

Building a church is not about attracting crowds; it is about the Lordship of Jesus Christ. If the first-century church needed a powerful book of Acts experience, how much more does our present generation need that same sold-out, unashamed church today?

Only the power of God working through a called and anointed minister preaching the Word of God with love, passion, and commitment; can bring about the change that causes men and women to turn from their sins and embrace the love of God for their souls.

Only those who fall in love with the Lord Jesus Christ—and not just in love with what He can do for them—will ever become true disciples.

We do not have to be harsh or mean to be true to the call of God. However, we must be firmly convinced that the gospel of Jesus Christ is the only message that will save the lost and give them entrance into the kingdom of God.

Paul emphasized this in his letter to the Galatian church:

> *But even if we, or an angel from heaven, preach any other gospel to you than what we have preached to you, let him be accursed. As we have said before, so now I say again, if anyone preaches any other gospel to you than what you have received, let him be accursed. (Galatians 1:8–9)*

There are no shortcuts, quick fixes, or one-size-fits-all methods for revival. Revival comes through prayer, fasting, faithful preaching, and laboring in the place where God has called you. Knowing that He is the one who gives the increase.

Jesus' words in Matthew 7:21–23 should help us stay focused on Who has called us and what He requires.

> *Not everyone who says to Me, "Lord, Lord," shall enter the kingdom of heaven, but he who does the will of My Father in heaven. Many will say to Me in that day, "Lord, Lord, have we not prophesied in Your name, cast out demons in Your name, and done many wonders in Your name?" And then I will declare to them, "I never knew you; depart from Me, you who practice lawlessness! (Matthew 7:21–23)*

Preacher, seek to please the One who called you to be faithful in declaring His Word. Remember it is His approval that will count in the end. We will cover this in more detail later.

Chapter Three

THE SIFTING
PROCESS

*And the Lord said, "Simon, Simon! Indeed, Satan has asked for
you, that he may sift you as wheat. But I have prayed for you,
that your faith should not fail; and when you have returned to
Me, strengthen your brethren." (Luke 22:31–32)*

Peter felt confident in his ability to stand firm. When Jesus
told the disciples, "You will all fall away because of Me this
night," Peter declared, "Though they all fall away because of You,
I will never fall away!" The Lord said to Peter, "But I tell you,
this very night, before the rooster crows, you will deny me three
times." Peter protested, "Lord, even if I must die with you, I will
not deny you!" Jesus looked at him with compassion: "Simon,
Simon! Indeed, Satan has asked for you that he may sift you as
wheat. But I have prayed for you, that your faith should not fail.
And when you have turned again, strengthen your brothers."

The metaphor Jesus used here is significant. In those days,
ripened wheat was spread on a floor of hard-packed earth—the

threshing floor. Then the farmer would begin the "sifting" process. Using a wooden flail, he would beat the wheat to separate the chaff from the edible grain. Jesus warned Peter he was about to go through a test much like the violent sifting of wheat. With compassion, Jesus assured Peter that He had prayed for him and when Peter had passed the test, he was to strengthen his brethren.

Jesus' warning did not prevent Peter from going through the sifting process.

What can we learn from this? *Everyone God uses will undergo the sifting process.* Like wheat that has grown accustomed to the outer shell, we come to God with the chaff of our self-will and self-sufficiency clinging stubbornly to our soul and spirit. The only way the precious wheat can be set free is to go through the intense sifting process.

Peter was too valuable to be sheltered from this. If he was wheat, then he had to be sifted in order to be useful. Peter would later write, "Think it not strange concerning the fiery trial that is to try you" (I Peter 4:12), and "God resists the proud but gives grace to the humble" (I Peter 5:5).

Satan has permission to dwell in the realm of darkness. He can traffic in any area of darkness that exists in a Christian's life. Any area that is not surrendered to Christ, any attitude, habit, or thought that is not in agreement with the nature of Christ or in harmony with the Word of God, will give the devil an opportunity to work against us.

The difficulties and testing we face are as necessary to our growth and benefit as sifting is to wheat.

After the wheat is sifted, it is then put through the winnowing process. Winds of temptations will blow across the winnowing floor of our lives. These winds may carry lightweight souls away, while the strong are stripped of their pride and self-confidence. The question from the winnowing floor is, "Does any chaff still cling to the wheat?"

Wheat may only need one round of sifting and winnowing to make it useful, but that is often insufficient for us. Disciples must be sifted and winnowed many times to make them fit for the Master's use. New tests, like finer mesh sieves, come their way to blow away the chaff of self-will, pride, and ego. As in Peter's case, being forewarned of these tests does not exempt ministers from experiencing them. Below is a list of several key areas in which you may be sifted:

(1) The area of change: One day everything seems to be going well for you and your family. But one phone call or one unexpected event can suddenly turn your world upside down. For example, you go from being well off and financially secure to being without any visible means of support. How will you deal with that? Job knew something about sudden and unexpected change when everything he had was taken from him in one single day.

On the other hand, you may struggle for a while with a lack of resources, but a sudden turn of events presents you with a financial windfall almost too good to be true. Will one change rob you of your faith and the other of your humility?

Paul was able to write, "For I have learned in whatever state I am, to be content: I know how to be abased, and I know how to abound. Everywhere and in all things, I have learned both to be full and to be hungry, both to abound and to suffer need. I can do all things through Christ who strengthens me" (Philippians 4:11–13).

Notice Paul "learned to be content" in numerous and varied circumstances. If this great apostle had some lessons to learn about the ups and downs of life, you too will need to learn them. Although you were unaware of it, you too had chaff still clinging to you when you answered the call of God to enter the ministry.

You may start off with great expectations and zeal as you accept the pastorate of a church or endeavor to start a new church. A few people from the area may stop by to check out the new pastor and attend the church for a while, causing you to think, *We're having revival! At this rate, it won't be long until we will need a bigger facility!* But think again. They can just as easily and unexpectedly move on without a word, leaving you wondering if you might have been out of the will of God all along.

You try everything you know to attract a crowd, fill the building, and keep them coming back. You invest your time, money, tears, your heart, and your soul into people only to see them walk away distracted by the cares of life, offended over the demands of true discipleship, then choose to attend another church down the road. All of this hurts and cuts deeply into the heart of a sincere pastor. However, if you think, *after all I have done to help these people, this is the way they treat me,* you could still have the chaff of pride clinging to you. Remember, my dear brother or sister, this is His church not yours or mine. This is not about us but all about Him. In time you will realize everyone is sifted and only those who fall in love with Jesus Christ will stay true to Him.

You can plant and water but only God can give the increase. You try your best to be kind, caring, and supportive, yet you must also stand for the truth of the Word of God and let Him do the sifting.

You are only the messenger trying to point people toward Jesus Christ. The choice is between them and the Lord. One consolation I have found is to remember, "If I can't take all the credit, then I won't take all the blame." People can be fickle and unpredictable at times, which should make you truly appreciate the faithful and committed people God has placed around you.

(2) *The area of character*: Character is the quality of becoming more like Christ as you deal with life, people, and the changing circumstances you encounter along the way. How will you respond to an offense, a wounded spirit, or the betrayal of your trust? How will you deal with disappointment, criticism, or misunderstanding? Your integrity, your word, and your honor all will be sifted on the threshing floor of life again and again. This can be very troubling when you encounter others without integrity. You may even be tempted to act the same toward them. Consider the following words of Michael Josephson (inspirationboost.com) about keeping your character in proper focus regardless of what others may do or say:

People of character do the right thing even if no one else does, not because they think it will change the world but because they refuse to be changed by the world.

---

(3) The area of motives: Jeremiah 17:9 reminds us that "the heart is deceitful above all things, and desperately wicked: who can know it?" Only God sees us as we really are. He desires to show us where we need to surrender to His Lordship and sovereign will. Like every minister, you want to do a great work for the Lord, but only time will reveal your true motives for being in the ministry. The sifting will reveal if you are convinced God has called you and you will continue through the good times and the bad until He directs you to do otherwise. You must be anchored by your relationship with Him and not the recognition or results you may or may not see.

I recall that in the first church I pastored a young man came to me one day and shared a letter explaining how a person could turn fifty dollars into several thousand by sending ten dollars to five people and placing their name at the bottom of the list. All he had to do was wait a while for this chain letter to pass through enough hands until his name was at the top of the list. According to the letter, it was legal. The young man was convinced it was an easy way for the church to raise money, which we always seemed to need. I didn't know whether or not it was legal, but I told the young man I didn't feel it was right for us to get involved in something like that. A few days later, the local newspaper ran an article exposing this chain letter scam and how it violated the law. It included a list of some names of the individuals that were involved. I was thankful the Lord had nudged me to avoid dragging the church into such a scandal. As I prayed about this, I felt the Lord prompt me that the real motive behind all of this was greed, not a desire to profit the work of the Lord. It is sad that some people who lost fifty dollars they could ill afford to lose would not think of putting that much in the offering. Motives can be buried under a lot of words and a deceitful heart, but God has a way of exposing our motives so they become pure and not self-seeking.

(4) The area of servanthood: Servants in biblical times did not have the negotiating power of unions. Indeed, they had no rights of their own. When it came down to when and how they served, it was entirely up to their master. Jesus identified Himself as one who came to minister rather than be ministered to. He laid down His will and His life to the will of His heavenly Father. We are called to follow in His steps. The call to the ministry is a call to serve the Lord first and then His people. Jesus did not die on the cross and call us into the ministry to provide us with a job or vocation. We are called to servanthood. Someone said, "You will never know if you have a servant's heart . . . until someone treats you like a servant."

In a small church, the minister and his family will often have to do all the chores that get done around the place. We have spent our share of time cleaning up rented halls, setting up chairs and equipment, trying to get everything in place and presentable for Sunday service. Then after service we would take it all down and load it up to carry home until next time.

I have also spent a lot of time working around the church when there was no one else willing or available to do the work. You can develop a negative attitude when you discover not everyone is as committed as you are. If you are going the extra mile, expecting others to recognize and appreciate your efforts enough to follow your example, you will be sadly disappointed. It is part of the sifting to find out who you really are serving and why.

What makes the work you are doing important is not where you serve. It is important because of the One who has called you to do it.

(5) *The area of patience*: Seldom do the promises of God come to pass as quickly as we had hoped. It seems like everything worthwhile takes longer than we planned or expected.

God promised Abraham a son, but twenty-five years passed before Isaac was born. It might have been less stressful if God had waited until the twenty-fourth year to promise Abraham that Sarah would bear him a son. That would have removed the element of faith and trust while Abraham waited on God. Sarah got tired of waiting and came up with her own solution to the problem by urging her husband to have a child by her handmaid Hagar. That was not God's plan, and it created a problem and conflict much worse than the waiting did.

Waiting on the Lord to answer a prayer or fulfill a promise or vindicate your ministry is never easy. You can easily feel frustrated and may be tempted to devise your own plan of trying to help God to see the promise fulfilled. When God opens the door, He doesn't need a battering ram. His timing is always perfect.

I have heard it said, "Faith is when you think God has had plenty of time to do something and He hasn't done anything yet, as far as you can tell." Waiting on God is definitely part of the sifting process for us to come to the place of absolute surrender and trust in Him.

What has Satan to do with the sifting process?

The devil is anxious to see if he can turn you away from trusting and obeying the Lord. He is pretty sure you won't pass the test. Remember his power and abilities are limited by the hand of God. For example, Satan was limited by God in his attack upon Job. At first, Satan mistakenly thought the hedge around Job was there to protect his position and possessions. Yet after everything he had was gone, Job still loved God and hated evil. Satan went back to God and asked for permission to take away Job's health. He said, "Skin for skin! All that a man has he will give for his life. But stretch out your hand and touch his bone and his flesh, and he will curse you to your face" (Job 2:4–5, ESV). Soon after, Job began to suffer from boils—not just one, but all over his body. Still he maintained his integrity before God. Integrity was the hedge around him, and God wouldn't let Satan tear it down. Let that hedge be around your life as well.

PETER'S MISSION

We might think after Peter denied the Lord three times, his influence and effectiveness in ministry would be completely gone. Perhaps the best he could hope for was to be forgiven and continue to live out his life in obscurity somewhere, haunted by the shadow of shame. We might ask, "How could such a man recover and be used of God?"

Peter's comeback was because Jesus had prayed for him that his faith would not fail in the hour of his testing. Jesus told him, "When you are converted, Peter, when you realize you are not as strong as you thought you were, when you have regained your bearings and turned back to Me, then I have a mission for you: strengthen the brethren, strengthen the believers."

On the shores of Galilee Jesus restored Peter when He asked, "Do you love Me?" Three times Jesus pressed him for his response. In humility and honesty Peter replied, "Yes, Lord, I have failed you and disappointed myself as well as others, but Lord, you know I love you." "Then feed my sheep," was the Master's instruction to him.

A ministry with any effectiveness is most often born out of adversities, failure, and hardships. You will minister and help other people most effectively in the areas where you yourself have received ministry and help.

The prophet Ezekiel said, "I sat where they sat" (3:15). Those called into the ministry are not kept from the tests and trials that are common to man. The lessons we learn about ourselves and about God are the very things that enable us to minister to others with compassion and understanding.

The Lord was not through with Peter; he was restored, and God used him to open the door to the church on the Day of Pentecost. He was later able to take a beating and rejoice that he was counted worthy to suffer for Jesus.

Peter had a lot of things sifted out of him: pride, self-confidence, rash presumption, and impulsiveness. When the process was complete, he was a powerful and effective minister.

Peter's fall and recovery has been a source of strength to many who may have in some way faltered and denied the Lord. As seen in his writings, this experience left an impression and changed Peter's outlook and his manner of ministering to people. He acquired humility and compassion. He learned to place confidence not in himself but in God. He gained wisdom and learned to wait patiently upon God through the sifting and winnowing process.

Peter must have been thinking of Jesus wrapping Himself in a towel and washing the feet of His disciples when he wrote, "Be clothed with humility, for 'God resists the proud, but gives grace to the humble'" (I Peter 5:5). He concluded this letter, "But may the God of all grace, who called us to His eternal glory by Christ Jesus, after you have suffered a while, perfect, establish, strengthen, and settle you. To Him be the glory and the dominion forever and ever. Amen" (I Peter 5:10–11). He pointed everyone to the true source of strength . . . Jesus Christ.

We are sifted and tested so we might be set free from the chaff of pride and self-sufficiency. Only then can we truly minister to others in their time of testing and difficulties.

Chapter Four

WOUNDED BY FRIENDLY FIRE

The spirit of a man will sustain his infirmity; but a wounded spirit who can bear? (Proverbs 18:14) And one shall say unto him, What are these wounds in thine hands? Then he shall answer, Those with which I was wounded in the house of my friends. (Zechariah 13:6)

When the military inadvertently causes damage to their own troops or allies, they refer to it as "friendly fire." However, the term doesn't make it less damaging or hurtful. When a person is injured, the body can't tell the difference: whether it was friendly fire or enemy fire, or how the injury took place. The person is wounded nonetheless. Soldiers expect to be shot at by their adversaries, but when they are shot by one of their own soldiers, it is extremely difficult to bear. How could they be so careless? Who was responsible for the mistake? How can it be avoided in the future? These questions are after the fact, and unfortunately, do not help the injured heal any quicker.

The Bible addresses this issue of spiritual wounds and broken hearts. For example:

I am poor and needy, and my heart is wounded within me. (Psalm 109:22)

He heals the brokenhearted and binds up their wounds. (Psalm 147:3)

The Spirit of the LORD *is upon Me, because he has anointed Me to preach the gospel to the poor; he has sent Me to heal the brokenhearted. (Luke 4:18)*

These wounds are most often caused by the unexpected words or actions of others: "For in many things we offend all. If any man offend not in word, the same is a perfect man, and able to bridle the whole body" (James 3:2).

The Word of God tells us every Christian will encounter offenses. All of us at one time or another will either be offended or will be the cause of an offense toward someone else. Our response to an offense will determine our future.

We live in a world of brokenhearted and wounded people. People who come to the Lord often come injured by divorce, abuse, neglect, abandonment, or betrayal. These wounds are often deeply entrenched in their minds, making them difficult for many to recognize. The wounds have become what Paul referred to as *strongholds* (II Corinthians 10:4–50), which are thoughts, imaginations, and arguments that are contrary to the Word of God and the nature of Jesus Christ.

Being called into the ministry does not exempt us from the painful encounters and experiences of living in an imperfect world with imperfect people just like ourselves. Unjust criticism, misunderstanding, careless and unkind words, or betrayal may come from those in your congregation—people you love and are trying your best to serve. Even worse, they can come from a fellow minister. Thus it is wise to expect to be wounded in your spirit, but even more important, know how to deal with it so you can help others heal from their wounds and broken hearts.

Many try to hide or bury their past hurts and wounds, but there are often tell-tale symptoms that may indicate a wounded spirit is unhealed. Let's look at nine of the symptoms:

(1) *A negative and critical mindset*: One who always sees the bad in everything and chooses to ignore the good usually is suffering from an unhealed wound. First responses are always negative: "That plan won't work; it will either take too long to implement or it won't last long enough; it is either too comprehensive or not comprehensive enough," and so on.

(2) *A victim mentality*: This is characteristic of people who regard themselves as sufferers at the hands of everyone else. They can turn even the kindest actions into a cause for grievance.

(3) *Blame tactics*: People who feel miserable and unhappy and are always blaming someone else probably have unhealed wounds. They may change churches, jobs, cities, or spouses, but they are convinced the problem is coming from any source but themselves.

(4) *Loss of joy*: Down-in-the-mouth people may still dutifully fulfill their obligations, but there is no joy in their service, no longer any awe or wonder about living for the Lord.

(5) *Withdrawal*: These are people who hold themselves aloof and avoid friendships for fear of being hurt again.

(6) *Sadness*: Memories haunt these people, causing deep pain like a festering wound. Certain situations stir their emotions and terrify them.

(7) *Easily offended*: When a person has unhealed wounds, it doesn't take much to cause them to feel a lot of pain or anger.

(8) *Believing lies*: The devil tells them what a bad person they are, that they are doomed to failure and rejection so they may as well give up trying. They are driven to ask themselves, "How can God possibly love a person like me?"

(9) *Lack of love*: Unhealed wounds rob these people of the ability to love and care for others as they should. Love requires closeness and vulnerability, things a wounded spirit fears the most.

God can heal spiritual wounds instantaneously, but for many, healing comes incrementally.

God can heal spiritual wounds in an instant and can deliver from any and all things. Yet for many, healing often comes incrementally. The process is not always easy, but it is necessary for our complete healing. In her article "Spiritual Healing: Three Biblical Steps to Heal Your Wounds" (ibelieve.com), Renee Davis lists these three steps: cleanse the wound, protect the wound and monitor the wound.

(1) *Cleanse the wound*: "If we confess our sins, He is faithful and just to forgive us our sins and to cleanse us from all unrighteousness" (I John 1:9).

Our infant daughter suffered third degree burns down her side and leg from scalding water. The doctor did not give us much

42

hope that she would survive the injury. She underwent multiple skin grafts over the next several years. Before the doctor could begin with the grafting, there was a process of debridement when damaged and dead tissue had to be removed to allow clean and healthy tissue to receive the graft. It was a painful ordeal for both our daughter and for her mother and I to go through, but it was necessary.

Just as a physical wound must be cleansed before it can begin to heal, our spiritual wounds need cleansing. And that can be a painful process. While our wound may be caused by the actions of others, we can be the cause of our own spiritual damage by how we respond. Unforgiveness is at the root of long-term spiritual wounds. Our cleansing must start with prayer. We must ask God to help us through the process of forgiving those who have hurt us and to help cleanse and remove the pain and hurt that has kept our wound from healing. It may also involve asking God to help us forgive ourselves.

When we forgive, God purges us from bitterness, strife, resentfulness, hurt, anger, guilt, and self-pity, all of which are spiritual toxins that have kept the wound from healing. We must make the choice to forgive in order to be healed.

In his book, *The Bait of Satan*, John Bevere offers the following insights about forgiveness:

- It is not an option: "If you do not forgive men their trespasses, neither will your Father forgive your trespasses" (Matthew 6:15)

- It does not make what happened OK.

- It releases the debt owed to you: "Forgive us our debts, as we forgive our debtors" (Matthew 6:12).

What steps can one take to cleanse a spiritual wound?

- Confess to God you are holding an offense—a wounded spirit toward another (Matthew 6:12).

- Admit your own sin in harboring the offense (Matthew 18:32–35).

- Forgiveness is an act of the will, after which you must focus on your healing rather than on your hurt (Ephesians 4:32).

(2) *Protect the wound*: "He heals the brokenhearted and binds up their wounds" (Psalm 147:3). Just as a physical wound requires a dressing to cover and protect it while it is healing, we must protect the wound while God is healing us. Our hurt may be caused from what others have said or done or perhaps from what we have brought on ourselves. If we choose to remain focused on our own pain, we are keeping the wound open because we are dwelling on our hurt instead of believing God for our healing.

Forgiveness requires that we stop focusing on our past hurts and injuries and focus on our healing. I have heard it said, "You can't change anything until you change your mind." How true! In order to protect the wound from being reopened again and again, you must choose to replace the destructive thoughts that you harbored before. This is done by allowing the Word of God to replace the old thought patterns. "Be not conformed to this world: but be ye transformed by the renewing of your mind"

(Romans 12:2). When anything triggers the memories of past injuries, rather than replaying the events over again, choose to stop that train of thought. Rather confess, "Lord I have forgiven that person and what they did and I refuse to pick it up and rehearse it again. I know You are my healer and that I am no longer a prisoner of the past." Then begin to speak the Word and promises of God over the situation. Here are a few verses to personalize to get started:

- "And ye shall know the truth and the truth shall make you free" (John 8:32).

- *I know the truth, you have set me free from my past. I am free now to forgive, free to love and free to worship without guilt or condemnation.*

- "Thou wilt keep him in perfect peace whose mind is stayed on thee" (Isaiah 26:3)

- *When I feel troubled let me remember your love and forgiveness for me. I claim your peace over my life and my thoughts right now.*

- "He sent his word and healed them" (Psalm 107:20). *Your Word brings healing to my mind and spirit. Let me hide it in my heart. Let me speak it in my prayer and worship. I am choosing to focus on your healing rather than my past hurts, in Jesus' name.*

(3) *Monitor the wound*: "Be sober, be vigilant; because your adversary the devil, as a roaring lion, walketh about, seeking whom he may devour" (I Peter 5:8). If we want our wounds to heal completely, we not only must continue the process of cleansing

and protecting, but we also must monitor our wounds closely for signs of infection. The enemy wants us to dwell on the injustices we have endured and to infect us with more anger, hurt, and doubt regarding our healing.

As mentioned above, we must forgive in order to be healed. Forgiveness involves releasing the record of offense we are holding against another. It is placing the offender in God's hands and not our own for settling the debt.

Even as they nailed Him to the cross, Jesus prayed, "Father forgive them; for they know not what they do" (Luke 23:34). But that did not mean those who rejected and crucified Him were reconciled to God.

Forgiveness was offered and is still extended to all who will come to God on the terms of the gospel. However, in order for us to receive forgiveness for our sins we must be willing to confess and turn away from them (I John 1:8–9). Then we can be reconciled with our heavenly Father. (See Colossians 1:19–23.)

We have the choice, as well as the commandment, to forgive those who wrong us, but the offender must also be willing to restore the relationship before there can be any reconciliation. That is why forgiveness is the choice of one person, but reconciliation also requires a choice and willingness on the part of the offender to restore harmony and relationship. Again, forgiveness involves one person—you; reconciliation requires two or more.

I have counseled individuals who have suffered because of the actions of family or friends through alcohol, drug addictions, or other destructive habits. God has helped them to forgive those individuals but that does not mean the other party has changed his or her habits or attitude necessary to restore the relationship. This lack of response does not bring closure or healing to the relationship as much as it may be desired. One must realize that they have little control over other people's actions. You are responsible for your conduct and attitude alone. Hopefully, with time and continued prayer they will change both their attitude and actions but it is their choice to make.

No matter how deep the wound or how long you may have suffered, Jesus knows what it is like to be wounded by those he loved and is ready and able to help with the healing process.

> *"But he was wounded for our transgressions, he was bruised*
> *for our iniquities: the chastisement of our peace was upon him;*
> *and with his stripes we are healed."* (Isaiah 53:5)

As a minister you will deal with hurting and wounded people more often than you would imagine. Hurting people tend to hurt other people. Pray for discernment to distinguish between the symptoms and the root problem. Often, people don't fully realize why they act or react the way they do. The lessons you learn and work through yourself will equip you to effectively minister to others, who have been wounded by friendly fire.

Chapter Five

TAKING ANOTHER LOOK AT SUCCESS

This book of the law shall not depart out of thy mouth; but thou shalt meditate therein day and night, that thou mayest observe to do according to all that is written therein: for then thou shalt make thy way prosperous, and then thou shalt have good success. Have not I commanded thee? Be strong and of a good courage; be not afraid, neither be thou dismayed: for the LORD thy God is with thee whithersoever thou goest. (Joshua 1:8–9)

Joshua was about to step into the shoes of Moses as the next leader of Israel. His mission was to bring the people into the Promised Land. God gave Joshua instructions on how to make his way prosperous and have good success. The instructions didn't come from a book on military strategies or a book on how to manage a multitude, but He did give him a book—the Word of God. If Joshua would immerse himself in the Word of God day and night, he would find everything he would ever need and find a solution for every problem he would ever face. Then God would prosper his way and he would have good success!

Success—isn't that what every pastor wants?

Success—isn't that what every pastor wants? Success is a popular subject, as seen in the hundreds of books purchased with titles like *How to Be a Leader Everyone Wants to Follow*, *How to Grow Your Church*, or *How to Reach Your Community*. I have a shelf full of books on different aspects of ministry and have found some helpful ideas in many of them. However, it has been my experience that there is no one-size-fits-all program for growing a church or being regarded as a successful pastor. Pastors face a tremendous amount of pressure along with some unrealistic expectations people may place on them, not to mention those they place on themselves. They are expected to be and do a myriad of things:

- Be spiritually deep and theologically wise

- Be a skilled public speaker

- Be a sensitive and wise counselor

- Be an adept manager and leader

- Be a diplomat

- Be a fund-raiser

- Be a committee chairperson

- Be a crisis manager, teacher, evangelist, and maintenance supervisor

- Be a comforter of the sick and bereaved

- Be a recruiter of new members

- Be able to lift up the discouraged

- Be an officiator at weddings, funerals, and other special occasions

- Be a representative of the church at public functions

All of this is a tall order to expect from anyone.

If your success in the ministry is measured by the size of your church building, the number of people sitting on the pews, and the amounts totaled up in the annual budget, you can easily become discouraged and disillusioned with your performance and results.

You may have gone to your city either to plant a church or to become pastor of an existing one. With high expectations, you began pouring yourself into the task set before you. But sometimes the results are not as great as your expectations. Often in your first attempt at pastoring, you discover that you "don't know what you don't know." This is because many things have to be learned by experience. Below are some examples of what I mean.

You are geared up for growth and revival with a vision of impacting your community. Your plans and the agenda are all laid out. When you try to implement the plans, you find that some of the church members have their own issues and agendas that knock them out of the running for the time being. You have to help them get through their problems before they are ready to help reach anyone else. To your disappointment, some may not last long enough for you to help them, and they drop out along the way.

Along with these unexpected setbacks, you find the bills are high and the income is low, so you try harder to make the best of what you have to work with. Discouragement can become an unwelcome and all-too-frequent companion, especially when a fellow pastor reports how a particular outreach worked for them, but when you try it, the results are less than spectacular.

Over the years I have seen a great number of different trends for church growth and evangelism. At one point, bus evangelism was the big thing. Churches bought old school buses and tried to fill them up with children—that is, if they could keep them running. Then came the Center of Interest trend where Sunday school students moved from teacher to teacher with different portions of the lesson and matching activities. However, that required more personnel than most churches had. Then there were small group and cell ministries, which are great ideas if you can create the climate and develop leaders to make it work.

Please don't misunderstand my point. I am not opposed to doing all we can to contact, attract, and retain visitors. I realize times have changed and our methods may need changing without changing our message. The reality is that every church is different. Not every congregation has the same talents and abilities. No two communities have the same demographics and dynamics. There is not a one-size-fits-all program you can copy.

How do you deal with the frustrations you feel when you try a program that worked elsewhere but did not work for you? There could be several reasons for this and I will share some insights in the next chapter.

If success is measured by how big, how many, and how much, you may feel like anything but a success. But don't despair; you are in good company. Let's take another look at success from the author and builder of the church and the men who walked with God through the pages of the Bible.

Noah, the man who found grace, worked on building the ark for one hundred and twenty years. While the ark "was a building," he preached to anyone who would listen that judgment was coming. Yet people refused to believe him. Even when the animals from far and near showed up and marched into the ark, the people didn't come. Noah ended up with only eight souls to show for his efforts. Had all that effort been worth the result?

Elijah, the man who rode in a chariot of fire, saw a great demonstration of God's power on Mount Carmel when the fire fell and consumed the sacrifice. He slew four hundred prophets of Baal and prayed until a downpour came after three years of drought. He then outran the king's chariot to the city. That was an impressive weekend! Still, the nation was unchanged. Jezebel threatened to kill him, and he fled for his life. Discouraged, despondent, and exhausted, he crawled under a juniper tree and told God he wanted to die. At that point, how do you think Elijah would have described his ministry?

Ezekiel, the man who saw the glory of God depart from Israel, heard a devastating word from the Lord: "Son of man, I will take away your dearest treasure. Yet you must not show any sorrow at her death. Do not weep; let there be no tears. Groan silently, but let there be no wailing at her grave. Do not uncover your head or take off your sandals. Do not perform the usual rituals of mourning or accept any food brought to you by consoling friends" (Ezekiel 24:15–17, NLT). The next evening Ezekiel's wife died. On this and many other occasions, God used Ezekiel as an object lesson to get a message to His people. This particular message was to warn them that they wouldn't be permitted to mourn the destruction of their beloved Temple. Yet Ezekiel's warnings went unheeded. The people persisted in their sin and rebellion against God until the Temple was destroyed. Ezekiel's ministry had at times been so thankless and unappreciated that God had to make his forehead as hard as flint. Do you think Ezekiel felt his ministry was successful?

Jeremiah, the weeping prophet, was an old man at the time of Ezekiel's ministry, and his message also had been rejected. The people hated Jeremiah so much that they mistreated him and even threatened his life; at one point they threw him in a miry pit and left him to die. God asked Jeremiah to do many strange things as a witness against the nation and their sins. This prophet's ministry spanned forty years, yet he never had one convert. How discouraging would that be?

John the Baptist, the forerunner of Christ, had a ministry so dynamic that it attracted great crowds. The stir he made condemning King Herod's sin resulted in a prison sentence. Alone in a dank dungeon, John began to wonder if his ministry had been a mistake. His depression was so deep that he even questioned Jesus' identity as Messiah. How could this be? John was the one who, when he saw Jesus approaching, had pronounced, "Behold the Lamb of God, which taketh away the sin of the world!" John sent two of his disciples to ask Jesus, "Are you the One, or should we look for another?" Jesus replied by pointing to all the miracles and wonders He was doing and then said, "Blessed is he that is not offended in me." After the two disciples left, Jesus told His followers there was no prophet greater than John the Baptist, but, as far as we know, John never heard those encouraging words. He understood that Christ must increase while he must decrease, but it didn't make his time in prison any easier. Do you think he felt successful?

My point is God measures success by a different standard than we do. God recognizes and places high value on things that might not occur to us. We might think talent or natural ability or charisma or oratory skill would be at the top of the list, but, surprisingly, God's list does not include things we can accomplish on our own. He places the greatest value on three qualities: a love for God, a servant's heart, and faithfulness.

OUR LOVE FOR GOD

The first and greatest commandment is to love God with all our heart, soul, strength, and mind (Luke 10:27). God requires that we love Him first and foremost. If we love preaching, position, recognition, or any other aspect of ministry above Him, we have missed the most important quality in God's sight.

In Revelation 2, John recorded the words of Jesus to the church in Ephesus, commending them for upholding the doctrine and for their good works. All of that faded from view when the Lord said, "Nevertheless I have somewhat against thee, because thou hast left thy first love." (Revelation 2:4). We can become so involved in the work of the Lord that we neglect the Lord of the work and our relationship with Him. I once read the following story, which powerfully illustrates how important Jesus must be in our lives:

> A minister told of a dream in which he was in a large room surrounded by the things associated with his life and ministry. There was the church he pastored and the official positions he held in his organization. He saw his wife and children, their home, and all the things they had acquired. Looking at all of it gave him a marvelous sense of self-satisfaction and accomplishment. Then Jesus came into the room and one by one began removing things. First, the Lord took the church and his ministry and his official positions out of the room, then He took his home and his possessions. Last, He took the minister's wife and children. Now the man was left alone in the room with Jesus. He heard the voice of the Lord say, "Is this enough? Am I all you need?" As the man struggled to comprehend what the dream meant and what the Lord was asking of him, he answered, "Yes, Lord, you are all I need." Jesus then said, "All right, I will bring all these things back into the room and into your life. I will let you have them, but remember they all belong to Me and I can take them at any time I choose."

What a sobering and thought-provoking experience that must have been! Yet how clearly it puts things in proper perspective. Our life and all the things that are associated with it belong to the Lord first and foremost. Our love for Him must be set above everything else we may have.

Imagine that everything in your life is going wonderfully well. You are happily married, you have five beautiful children, and a successful career. Then over a short period of time it is all taken away. How would you respond? Kenneth W. Osbeck's book, *101 Hymn Stories*, recounts the experience of Horatio Spafford, whose life was drastically changed:

> Horatio Spafford was a devout Christian, a church elder, and a prominent lawyer in Chicago in the mid-1800s. He was described by a noted gospel musician of that era as "a man of unusual intelligence and refinement, deeply spiritual, and a devoted student of the Scriptures." Spafford's business was thriving, so he invested in several real estate properties on the shore of Lake Michigan. Then in 1871, his four-year-old son died of scarlet fever. That same year, the Great Fire of Chicago wiped out his real estate investments. Osbeck states, "Desiring a rest for his wife and four daughters as well as wishing to assist D. L. Moody and Sankey in one of their campaigns in Great Britain, Spafford planned a European trip for his family in November 1873." However, unexpected business demands prevented him from accompanying his family, so he sent them ahead on the steamship *Ville du Havre*, with plans to join them later. Before this could happen, however, he received a cablegram from his wife, telling him the *Ville du Havre* had been struck by an iron sailing

vessel and all four of their daughters had perished. Grief stricken, Horatio hurriedly boarded a ship and set sail for Europe to rejoin his wife. During the voyage he passed over the area where his children had died. There he penned the timeless hymn that begins with the words:

When peace like a river
Attendeth my way,
When sorrows like seas billows roll;
Whatever my lot, Thou has taught me to say,
It is well, it is well, with my soul.

Not all of God's children have to walk through such a shockingly horrific valley. Spafford's hymn extolling the redemptive work of Christ and anticipating His glorious Second Coming proves that his love for the Lord was not just lip service. He lived it out in the good times and the bad. Even with a broken heart his faith was still intact as he wrote, "It is well with my soul." Jude admonished, "Keep yourselves in the love of God" (Jude 21). Your love for God and a desire to please and serve Him above all things will keep you anchored to His call no matter what circumstances or difficulties you may be going through at the time.

A SERVANT'S HEART

As the disciples prepared for the Last Supper they would share with their Master, they obtained a room, set everything up, and acquired all the necessary food, but omitted to procure someone to perform the customary foot-washing chore. It was a lowly task of a servant to wash the feet of guests who traveled the dusty roads and streets of the day. After the supper was ended, Jesus laid aside His garments, girded Himself with a towel, and, one by one, washed the disciples' feet. Afterward He said, "If I then, your Lord and Master, have washed your feet; ye also ought to wash one another's feet" (John 13:14).

On more than one occasion Jesus taught His disciples that servanthood was more highly esteemed in the kingdom of God than any position or title. "But he who is greatest among you shall be your servant" (Matthew 23:11). The ultimate act of service was at Calvary where Jesus laid down His life for us all.

We cannot separate our service to the Lord and our serving others. In fact, Jesus said, "Verily I say unto you, Inasmuch as ye have done it unto one of the least of these my brethren, ye have done it unto me" (Matthew 25:40).

It is important to remember you are the Lord's servant as you serve His people. People are sometimes ungrateful and forgetful. They can be petty and openly critical. If you are looking to people for your validation and worth, you may be very disappointed. You will never know if you have a servant's heart until someone treats you like a servant. You would do well to remember the words and example of our Lord: "The Son of Man did not come to be served, but to serve, and to give His life a ransom for many" (Matthew 20:28).

FAITHFULNESS

"Most men will proclaim each his own goodness, but who can find a faithful man?" (Proverbs 20:6). Some people can be inspired for the moment, but when the newness and excitement of serving God wears off and difficulties arise or when there seem to be more losses than gains, they get discouraged and drop out. The Scripture declares that one of the most difficult qualities to find is not talent or giftedness, but rather, it is faithfulness.

Faithfulness reminds us that some things in life call for patience, self-denial, and discipline. It speaks of the drudgery of plodding on at times when we feel like quitting. However, this unglamorous quality is held in the highest regard by God, who identifies Himself as the *Faithful Creator* and the *Faithful God* who keeps covenant. Faithfulness, steadfastness, and dependability are the very attributes of God Himself.

I have observed that when a man goes to a city to pastor a church, all he sees are possibilities. Over time however, he may lose sight of the possibilities and see only the liabilities. That is when we must focus our eyes on the Lord who called us into His service. Only then can we see things from His perspective.

God does not compare you to anyone else or your field of labor to anyplace else. You have a unique set of circumstances, season of life, and ministry. It is not fair to compare yourself, or the place you serve, with anyone else.

Additionally, you are not being held back by anything you lack materially to fulfill God's plan. Whenever God's servants stood perplexed by what the Lord was calling them to do, He simply asked, "What is in your hand?" For Moses it was a rod; for Samson it was a jawbone; for the widow it was a cruse of oil;

for the disciples it was five loaves and two fish. God uses what you have and what you offer to Him, and that is always sufficient. Be faithful with what God has entrusted into your hands at this season of your life and ministry. You are called to plant and water, but He is the One who gives the increase.

Faithfulness also includes obedience. When the Israelites complained they were thirsty, God told Moses to speak to the rock. Frustration made Moses feel more like hitting something than just speaking to it. After all, that's what previously had brought water out of the rock. So he struck the rock, and water came out. The people didn't care how the miracle was done; they just wanted to satisfy their thirst. However, God didn't think the end justified the means. That act of disobedience kept Moses from setting foot on the soil of the Promised Land. Perhaps that decision seems rather severe in our eyes, but the Scriptures teach, "From everyone who has been given much, much will be required, and from the one who has been entrusted with much, even more will be asked" (Luke 12:48, NET Bible). Moses had intimate encounters with God, and as a result God required much more from Moses. You and I have been entrusted with much; let us be careful that we fulfill our calling faithfully in all things.

Faithfulness involves obedience at every level.

If you measure your success by anything other than your love for God, having a servant's heart, and being faithful and obedient, you may become disillusioned and disheartened at the ebb and flow of church attendance and finances. You may not possess the organizational skill or the speaking ability or have the charismatic personality of others more gifted than you are. God called you, knowing what you had and did not have going for you. God knew where He would place you and what struggles and sifting He would bring you through in order to use you in a greater way. Still, you can be as good as the others in the three areas in which God measures success: you can love God with all your heart, mind, and strength, you can have a servant's heart, and you can be faithful to His call upon your life. The only commendation that will matter on the day when you stand before the Lord is to hear Him say, "Well done, thou good and faithful servant."

In the next chapter we will look at some of the seasons of ministry we pass through in following the call.

Chapter Six

THE SEASONS OF MINISTRY

To every thing there is a season and a time to every purpose under heaven. . . . He hath made all things beautiful in His time. (Ecclesiastes 3:I, II)

God has established the seasons of life and the changes that each season brings. Winter comes with its bone-chilling cold, barren trees, and quiet stillness of the snow-covered landscape, hiding all that is unsightly with its own sparkling beauty. This is followed by spring, when life is renewed, warm breezes melt the ice and snow, gentle rains water the ground, colorful flowers bloom, and the spreading tree limbs are bursting with buds. What a welcome change from winter! This is followed by summer, when the sunlight warms the earth, inviting us to come outdoors to enjoy the longer days and relaxing times. But all too soon that warmth and enjoyment give way to fall—the early frost paints the leaves brilliant colors before the chill winds blow them to the ground. It's time for bountiful harvests, bright orange pumpkins, apple cider, and hay mazes. But fall bows to the cold winds of winter, and the cycle begins again. Each season has its beauty and benefits as well as its storms and undesirable weather, but we can rest assured that each season will pass with time.

When one accepts the call of God to enter the ministry, he or she enters a seasonal process of development and maturing. The cycle is a common rite of passage that all ministers must pass through. The seasons of ministry come and go in the same manner as the natural seasons of life.

David was chosen by God and anointed by Samuel to be king over Israel, but he was not crowned and enthroned on that momentous day. God knew David needed to be sifted and endure the winnowing process of time and life experiences before he was ready to shoulder such a responsibility. Throughout life's seasons, he learned how to trust God to fight his battles. He learned how to dodge spears thrown at him by a jealous and fearful father-in-law without becoming bitter and vengeful. When he had the advantage and opportunity and even encouragement from others to take matters into his own hands and destroy Saul, David refused to harm the Lord's anointed.

When David fled for his life to the cave of Adullam, the Scripture records, "Everyone who was in distress, and everyone who was in debt, and everyone who was discontented gathered to him" (I Samuel 22:2). These four hundred men were a disgruntled, unhappy lot without much promise or future. But as they spent time with David, his character and integrity began to affect them in positive ways, and they became known as David's mighty men, accomplishing great exploits of heroism and valor.

After the death of King Saul, David was anointed king over the tribe of Judah in Hebron where he ruled for seven years. Only then did God deem he was finally ready to be crowned king over the entire nation of Israel as God had promised years before.

David's ascent to the throne took time, but those seasons of David's life and ministry were a necessary process. Against the backdrop of David's life experiences, I would like to share with you three seasons of ministry regarding this process. First, God develops the man; second, God develops the people following the man; and third, God develops the circumstances around the man.

These seasons of ministry cannot be rushed through or controlled. When the apostles asked Jesus if He planned to restore the kingdom of Israel before He ascended, Jesus replied, "It is not for you to know the times or the seasons which the Father hath put in his own authority" (Acts 1:7).

When we first acknowledge the call of God, He will often give us a preview of what He wants to do with our lives. This can be both exciting and a little frightening as we realize how inadequate and unprepared we are to do such things, but as we pass through the seasons of ministry, God will prepare and equip us for His service. Just as the seasons return each year, so will the seasons of personal growth, the development of those around us, and our submission to God's orchestration of our circumstances to bring about His plan and purpose. We must never stop growing or try to remove ourselves from the seasonal cycle as He perfects His nature and will in our lives.

Just as the seasons return each year, so will the seasons of personal growth, the development of those around us, and our submission to God's orchestration of our circumstances to bring about His plan and purpose.

FIRST, GOD DEVELOPS THE MAN

It has already been said, "God does not call the qualified; He qualifies the called." In other words, He doesn't see what we are, but what we can become. However, I would like to point out that neither does He ignore or overlook what we are when He calls us. The potter forms the clay on the wheel until it is just as he desires. He then fires it in the kiln to cure and become a vessel fit for service, so God places those He will use on His potter's wheel, working out the imperfections until they yield to the work of His hands. He then tests his work by the fires of sifting, wounding by friends, adversity, temptation, and troubles that are common to man.

We cannot readily see our blind spots of pride, selfishness, or ego, but the Potter sees them clearly. Skillfully and thoroughly, the Potter works to develop the man into a vessel He can use. Peter cautioned, "Think it not strange concerning the fiery trial which is to try you" (I Peter 4:12). Every minister will go through his or her own fiery trials; they will face financial difficulties, sickness, disappointments, sorrow, hurt, and dark days of loneliness and misunderstanding as they learn to depend completely upon the Lord for all things and not upon their own talent and abilities.

These are the same experiences life brings to everyone. Those called of God must know firsthand the struggle and the trying of their own faith as well as the victory that comes to those who love and trust the Lord in order to minister effectively to others. The prophet Ezekiel was addressing this concept when he remarked, "I sat where they sat" (Ezekiel 3:15). He was made to partake of the captivity and suffering of the exiles so he could minister to them more effectively.

Jesus told Peter, "Satan has asked for you, that he may sift you as wheat. But I have prayed for you, that your faith should not fail; and when you have returned to Me, strengthen your brethren" (Luke 22:31–32). The purpose of Peter's testing was to purify his character and strengthen his faith so he would be able to minister to others. (See chapter 3.) We will be called to go through these seasons in order to develop a heart of compassion and a testimony of God's grace to impart and minister to others who are going through their own tests and trials.

God does not call us into the ministry after we are perfectly mature and have learned all of life's lessons. While we are called to teach, we are still learners; while we are called to lead, we are still learning to follow Him. Paul acknowledged that he had not yet arrived but was still pressing toward the mark and goal that was before him. This season of God developing the man is an ongoing process.

I was only twenty-nine when I was elected to my first pastorate. I did not have much experience or preparation to pastor a congregation. All I had to offer was a sincere desire to do my best for the Lord. I endeavored to preach and teach, but looking back on some of my notes, my sermons were not very deep. I have often prayed, God, please bless those faithful saints I practiced on! And Lord, please make up for all my feeble attempts to deal with the drama, the pettiness, and the crisis management I suddenly found myself swirling in.

Mistakenly, I thought I had to solve every problem people brought to me and find a way to help everyone out of the financial crises they got into. I would worry and fret over the uncommitted and careless. I tried my best to preach and reach for them and call them every time they missed a service. When they didn't change, I wondered what I was doing wrong.

I learned the hard way that God called me to be His messenger and as a pastor all I could do was to point people to Jesus Christ and give them biblical principles to live by. It was up to them to fall in love with and choose to follow Him. I also learned you can "over pastor" people. The saints didn't feel a need to depend upon God because I was always trying to help them get through their problems. By doing this, even though my efforts were sincere, I was robbing them from learning to depend on the Lord to meet their needs and keeping them from suffering the consequences of their poor choices.

I say this to point out that even though God had called me to pastor this little flock, He was still in the process of teaching me, revealing things to me, and developing me. I had to learn about myself, my calling, and what God's priority was for His church. I had to learn that the flock was not my own; they were His sheep. The priorities were not mine to choose; I must leave that up to Him.

Every inadequacy you have, every challenge that seems impossible, and every problem you face are the very opportunities God uses to cause you to turn to Him again and again for His grace, wisdom, and direction. You have been called to God-sized tasks that can only be accomplished through Him. Learn to turn to Him first—and not as a last resort. Don't despair about the seasons that come your way; you are on the Potter's wheel. He will mold and shape you with His hands, then when the time is right, He will place you in the fire of the kiln. Afterward, you are ready for Him to adorn you with masterful brush strokes of a colorful glaze, then He places you in the kiln again for the final firing. Understand through it all, God is developing you; the finished product is yet to be revealed.

SECOND, GOD DEVELOPS THE PEOPLE FOLLOWING THE MAN

David started out with a ragtag group of disgruntled, oppressed debtors and their families. They knew how to fight and could do that quite well. As they spent time with David, they learned why God would call him a man after His own heart. They watched how David dealt with Saul when he refused to take revenge upon a sworn enemy. They saw the value David placed on the men who risked their lives to break through the Philistine camp to bring him a drink of water from the well in Bethlehem. The people saw he was fair in sharing the spoils of war with those who guarded the camp as well as those who fought in the battle. They saw how David could be entreated when Abigail came and reasoned with him to prevent the slaughter of Nabal's household. No doubt the men around David heard his prayers and listened to his psalms of love and devotion and intercession to his God. He was not putting on a show; his actions were genuine.

As a newly elected pastor, it is important to realize you may have the title of pastor but it will take time for the people to make you *their* pastor and shepherd as they observe how you deal with your own struggles, and how you deal with other people. Your life and actions will speak louder than any sermon or Bible lesson you will deliver from a pulpit.

Edgar A. Guest captures this point in his poem:

SERMONS WE SEE

I'd rather see a sermon than hear one any day.
I'd rather one should walk with me than merely tell the way.
The eye is a better pupil, more willing than the ear;
Fine counsel is confusing, but example is always clear.
And the best of the preachers are the men who live their creeds,
For to see good put into action is what everybody needs.

I can soon learn how to do it if you will let me see it done;
I can watch your hand in action, but your tongue too fast may run.
And the lectures you deliver may be very wise and true,
But I'd rather get my lesson by observing what you do.
For I may misunderstand you and the high advice you give,
But there is no misunderstanding how you act and how you live.

When I see a deed of kindness, I am eager to be kind.
When a weaker brother stumbles and a strong man stands behind
Just to see if he can help him, then the wish grows strong in me
To become as big and thoughtful as I know that friend to be.
And all the travelers can witness that the best guide today
Is not the one who tells them, but the one who shows the way.

One good man teaches many; men believe what they behold;
One good deed of kindness noted is worth forty that are told.
Who stands with men of honor learns to hold his honor dear,
For right living speaks a language which to everyone is clear.
Though an able speaker charms me with his eloquence, I say,
I'd rather see a sermon than hear one any day. (*Public domain*)

It takes time to develop leaders, to strengthen and help the men and women around you to become equipped and confident that God can and will use them in His plan and purpose. People are the greatest variable you will have to deal with in the work of God. Trying to help them become spiritually mature, consistent in their walk with God, and to conduct themselves in a Christlike manner in every area of life, will not be accomplished with a single sermon or Bible lesson. It will require much time, effort, prayer and preaching for those who want to grow, to grasp, and put into practice what God's Word teaches and requires of us all.

Remember the people following you are God's children, His people, and His sheep. It was His blood and sacrifice that purchased salvation for all of us. Be careful how you treat them. When everyone is prayed up and spiritually right, they can be almost angelic; when they are carnally minded in their words and actions, watch out! The devil can do a lot of damage through carnally minded people, including preachers!

I remember a church where I served as the Sunday school director fresh out of Bible college. I tried to implement accountability and quality control regarding faithfulness and commitment like I had read about in the how-to books—without much success I might add. I called a staff meeting, intending to straighten them out . . . or so I thought. I wasn't praying for direction, as I was pretty sure I knew what needed to be done. But God in His own way came to talk with me. He asked, "Are you upset because these people are not doing what you expect of them or are you upset because they are not doing what I expect of them?" I was convicted of my pride and ego and asked God to forgive me. When I met with the staff, the mood was totally different than the meeting I had planned. God came down and there was

71

a renewed commitment from all of us to serve the Lord, not just to please the new Sunday school director.

Always keep in mind this is His church and His people. We are called to shepherd, guard, and guide them under His direction. They are not there for our agenda, dreams, or egos.

There will be times you will be frustrated, hurt, and disappointed with people and their actions. As my friend Bishop Ronnie Mullings is fond of saying, "People are pitiful and we are all people." So, thank God for those faithful and dependable folks He has placed around you. Encourage and minister to them. Love and preach to the others who are still struggling, trying to develop some consistency in their lives. Don't bring your negative attitudes to the pulpit; you won't help anyone, and you most likely will say things you will regret later. A seasoned minister once told me, "Never spank the whole church just because one or two need it." That's still good advice.

Over time, each church congregation will take on the passion, attitude, and character of their pastor. Someone once asked the question, "What kind of church would this church be if everyone in it was just like me?" Strive to be the best example of a Christian first, a husband and father second, and a minister and pastor last.

THIRD, GOD DEVELOPS THE CIRCUMSTANCES AROUND THE MAN

"The steps of a good man are ordered by the LORD: and he delighteth in His way" (Psalm 37:23). Yes, God is in control, even when we can't see how things will work out. Noah could have had a nervous breakdown worrying about getting the ark built before the rains came or how he was going to get all the animals inside, along with enough food to last indefinitely (God hadn't informed him of those details). We know from our vantage point that God had all of it in control. Admitting "God has it all in control" and actually living with that peace of mind are not always the same . . . especially when we're starting out in the ministry but He always does and you can count on that.

We live in a fast-paced world, one that admires the busy people with full agendas and crammed day-timers and appointment books. Beware the barrenness of busyness, my friend. Activity is not always synonymous with productivity. There are some things you simply cannot rush through or force to fit your agenda or make happen. God controls the seasons and the timing for our lives to fulfill His plan and purpose.

There is a time and a season for everything.

Before my wife and I married, we discussed our burden and desire to serve the Lord and found that we both felt we would someday be involved in missions work on a foreign field. At the time, we did not know where or when or how it would all come about, but we felt strongly that was the direction God had for us. After marriage, we served in various churches and positions in whatever capacity we were afforded, trusting God to open every door at the right time.

At one point I happened to read about a nearby church that had quite a large missions commitment for its size, and as I read the article a strange impression came over me that I would pastor that church one day. I had never even been to that church or met the current pastor. I was serving as a sectional Sunday school director, and this pastor contacted me to come and conduct a Sunday school training session for him. Afterward, he invited me to his home for a meal and began asking questions about my ministry and what I felt called to do. I told him that I felt called to pastor someday. He went on to ask me where and I felt extremely awkward in trying to tell him, but he continued to press me. I finally said, "I don't know how to explain this to you, sir, but I feel that I will one day pastor this very church." I had no idea he was already applying for a missionary appointment and would be leaving the country. Over the course of the next year, God orchestrated this man's life and my own, and I was elected to be the next pastor of that church. I could not have arranged these things; only God could bring it to pass, and He did it all in His time.

Eight years later my wife and I were sitting in a general conference in Salt Lake City when there was an appeal for China Outreach Radio Broadcast. China was still closed, but through radio the gospel was being sent into the country. I turned to my wife and said, "Wouldn't it be something if we were there when the door opens for China?" Little did either of us know how God would direct our steps. A year later we were on our way to Hong Kong under missionary appointment. Again, things like this can be brought to pass only by God.

Every man and woman of God called into His service will experience these three seasons of their ministry: God developing the individual, God developing the people around them, and God orchestrating the circumstances to bring about His will and purpose. I can testify to this in my own life as God has opened every door that we have walked through in our fifty years of ministry. You can rest assured, my friend, that He will do the same for you!

Chapter Seven

THE MINISTER'S FAMILY

For this cause shall a man leave his father and mother, and shall be joined unto his wife, and they two shall be one flesh. This is a great mystery: but I speak concerning Christ and the church. Nevertheless, let every one of you in particular so love his wife even as himself; and the wife see that she reverence her husband. (Ephesians 5:31–33)

God intended for marriage and the home to be a model of His relationship with the church. Most of us, as we start out in ministry, are young and still learning a lot about ourselves, marriage, and family. We certainly don't have it all together—I know I didn't. When we start out in life, we cannot know what we don't know; that is, many things are learned only by experience. The good news is we don't have to learn everything the hard way. Today there is an abundance of well-written books from Christian writers on just about every aspect of marriage and family. This is a subject you never graduate from. Just as the seasons of life change, you and your spouse under-go change, along with your children. We are constantly learning and adjusting or at least we should be, not only for our benefit but for the sake of those we love and minister to.

While some say their marriage was made in heaven, it still has to be lived out here on earth. A minister's home is not exempt from the tests and trials common to all families; in fact, there are additional pressures on the minister's home. It can be a real struggle at times trying to maintain a balance of responsibilities and demands from the family, the congregation, and often an outside job as well. The stress can be very real and intense. For that reason, we must safeguard our core values and relationships. The barrenness of busyness will not compensate for the neglect of our own soul or our own family.

The following thoughts on the minister's family are from lessons I have learned and observed over time. I sincerely hope you find some of them helpful.

1. Don't confuse "church work" with a relationship with the Lord. When you are too busy to pray, too busy to get alone with God, too busy for personal time with the Word of God, you are too busy! If not corrected, this busyness will inevitably lead to spiritual shipwreck and disaster. The call of God is a *spiritual* calling. The man of God must be a spiritual man or he is just going through the motions, regardless of the talents and abilities he may have.

That which is born of the flesh is flesh; and that which is born of the Spirit is spirit. (John 3:6)

If you depend on the arm of human flesh, you will get only what the flesh can provide; but if you depend on the Spirit, you have everything the Spirit of God can provide. Keep yourself in the love of God, preacher. The devil never takes a vacation. He goes about seeking whom he may devour. If he can trip up a preacher, he will—and in the process take down as many others as he can.

2. *Your family should be your first and greatest area of ministry.* Your family must not be sacrificed on the altar of your ministry. The salvation of your spouse and children are your greatest responsibility. The nature of the pastoral ministry often involves being called on in emergencies of all kinds. However, not every phone call is an emergency. Not every request to talk with you is urgent. It is a good idea to set some boundaries around your time and home. Set a day or evening that you have an appointment with your own family. If someone wants to see you or talk to you, just say you have a prior commitment. Your family will appreciate you placing them as a priority and will understand when real emergencies arise.

As much as possible, let your home be a place of refuge for your family, not just an extension of the church. Let people know your home is for fellowship and family, not for dealing with problems they may have. People often bring spirits and attitudes with them. You don't want your home to be open to unnecessary conflict and issues with people. Counsel people with problems somewhere outside your home, preferably at the church if possible. Most likely you will want the liberty to pray with them afterward, and the church allows that freedom.

3. Love is spelled T-I-M-E; make quality time for your wife. Make a date with your wife each week, even if it is only for lunch or coffee. Talk about your family and what is important to them. Celebrate and appreciate your wife; don't ever take her for granted. Let her know in every way possible how important and loved she is by you and God. Being a pastor's wife can be very lonely and a huge burden to carry at times. There are very few people she can open up and talk to. Don't let church, people, problems and challenges consume all of your thoughts and time. Your family deserves quality time with you as well. No one said it would be easy, but it is extremely important to be aware of this pitfall and work together to make the most out of special times together.

Regardless of how well a man may be thought of in public, you can often see in the face of his wife and children every deposit and withdrawal he has made in them. Guard your home! In doing so you will guard your life and ministry as well.

4. Make time for your own children and family. I recall the story of a young boy who was sitting on the front doorstep early one Saturday morning with his fishing pole and tackle box at the ready. His dad had promised to take him fishing. He was so excited they would be spending some time together. His dad always seemed so busy with everyone else that time alone with his dad was rare. The front door burst open and his dad came rushing out. It wasn't until the father spotted his son waiting with his fishing gear that he remembered his promise to his son. His shoulders slumped. "I'm sorry," he said, "but something has come up at the church and I have to meet someone this morning." The young boy staring at his dad heard him say, "Don't worry, son. We'll go fishing some other time." The little boy laid down the fishing gear and with an expression of disappointment and resentment watched his dad drive off.

When you make plans or promises to do things with your children, do all you can to keep those promises. You do not want them to grow up thinking people in the church are more important to you than they are. Teenage rebellion often comes from bitterness over a wounded spirit and broken promises.

It is important to spend time with your children individually as well as collectively. You are mentoring them to be disciples and followers of Jesus Christ. Stay aware of what is happening in their life and school, their friends and struggles. You are their dad as well as their pastor. Each child has unique gifts and talents that you want to help them cultivate and develop. Never compare your children with each other or with anyone else for that matter. That hurts and makes them feel they don't measure up to your expectations or merit your approval.

When they are very young and you are training them, be consistent in your discipline and rewards. You are human, so sometimes you may feel lenient and other times you may be short tempered and impatient. Your children need to know the rules of the house and you won't be changing those rules whenever the mood strikes you.

Children need to know the three D's—disobedience, dishonesty, and disrespect—are offenses that will be punished and corrected. Spilling their milk and being noisy should not be a capital offense, even if it is irritating. Remember your boy is not a man yet and your girl is not a woman. Don't measure their efforts and abilities by what you expect from yourself. Teach your children the how and why of things, Dad. Remember you have a heavenly Father who has a lot of patience with you too.

Daughters will get their sense of value at a young age from their father. Take them on a date. Compliment them and their mother often. Let them know they are special to you and that God has a plan and purpose for their lives. Before your children reach the dating stage, talk to them about dating and marriage and the qualities they value in life. It is a mistake to wait until they get emotionally involved with someone and then try to develop an open communication with them.

Let your children hear you pray and that you are praying for them. Don't relegate Christianity to something you do only at church. Talk about God's goodness, His provision and blessings every day. Don't let criticism, problems, and people be the topics of discussion in your home.

5. Teach your children from an early age to pray about their needs and desires. When my wife and I were serving as missionaries in Hong Kong, we had a very modest personal income. One year I felt to make a pledge for our Christmas for Christ offering back in the States. We did not have any money to spare. I told our daughters we should pray and ask God to supply the need. That year we received several checks in the mail amounting to the pledge we had made! To make the miracle of provision even more obvious, we had never received any personal checks before that time. It was a great lesson for our daughters to learn to trust God at an early age.

Guide your children in learning to work and save for things they want. We live in a society where many feel they are entitled to anything and everything they want ... at someone else's expense.

It is difficult for those raised in North America to relate to the poor standard of living in much of the rest of the world. We need to help our children understand how blessed and fortunate we are in North America and that we cannot take credit for being born and raised here. Part of their training and happiness should be doing things for others; teaching them it is truly more blessed to give than to receive.

6. *Keep your business affairs in order.* Taking care of your family involves more than feeding, clothing, and housing them while trying to live within your budget. The reality is we never know when the unexpected or unwelcomed events of life may intrude on our families and stretch our budget to the breaking point.

Preacher, I know by experience how important it is for young ministers to do all they can to provide for their family in the event of their unexpected death. Having insurance and a legal, up-to-date will is part of taking care of your family. I have known of families that when the husband passed away, they were left with hardly enough to cover funeral expenses. Some spouses have no idea about the family finances, bank accounts, passwords, and so on. The departed spouse has handled all of that and neglected to explain what to do if something happens to them. This compounds the tragedy unnecessarily. It is far better to have a plan and never need it than to need one and not have it.

I realize when starting out in pastoral ministry, not every church is self-supporting or has the means to set up a retirement fund for the pastor. Still, you should have a plan in place.

I have seen good men continue to pastor well past their prime and effectiveness because they needed the income from the church to live on. As a result, the church suffered. To a young man, retirement seems unreal and a long way off, but those years will come much sooner than one might expect. Again, it is better to have a plan and not need it.

Your plans will change and need adjustment as you pass through the various seasons of life. Purpose to be a good steward of the resources you have available to you. This is one more way to show your care for your spouse and family.

Your family is your greatest investment in the next generation so guard and keep it with utmost prayer and care. Enjoy each season of life with your family. Be fun to live with. Be the father your kids want to be around. Take mini vacations or just a day trip somewhere when resources are limited. Remember love is a four-letter word also spelled T-I-M-E.

Chapter Eight

ACCOUNTABILITY

In those days there was no king in Israel; everyone did what was right in his own eyes. (Judges 17:6)

The book of Judges records some of the most tragic and dark years in the moral history of Israel. After the death of Joshua and the elders who had come through the wilderness journeys, the next generation lacked any leadership or accountability for their actions. The Lord had given them commandments to live by so they would have His blessing and favor. Sadly, the record shows that without a leader the people drifted far from God whenever they were left to themselves. Only when God permitted their enemies to oppress them did they repent and seek His mercy and forgiveness. Then the Lord would raise up leaders (called judges) to deliver the people from their oppressors. The people served the Lord as long as they had a godly leader; however, when that leader passed off the scene, the nation would drift away from God. The cycle was repeated time and time again throughout the period of the judges. For about three hundred years, *every man did that which was right in his own eyes.*

Northcentral Idaho, where I live, abounds with beautiful mountains, rivers, and canyons. Freeways and interstates are rare. In fact, there are many two-lane roads winding up and down the mountains with guardrails to prevent travelers from plunging over the side into the canyons or riverbeds. It is obvious these guardrails won't stop a car from crashing through them if the driver is careless. They are there simply to warn a driver that he is veering too close to the edge.

One night while driving up a steep grade, I became caught in a snowstorm. The higher I climbed the worse the visibility developed until I found myself in a complete whiteout. The only thing I could see that gave me any idea where the road lay before me were the small reflectors mounted on the guardrail beside the road. I couldn't see the road, but I knew where it was supposed to be. I also knew when it curved and where the edge of the road was. I continued driving with extreme caution, keeping an eye on the reflectors along the way until I crested the top and dropped back into the valley below where the visibility was much better.

Proverbs 21:2 reminds us, "Every way of a man is right in his own eyes: but the LORD pondereth the hearts." Accountability is like the guardrail keeping us from straying off the road and avoiding the consequences.

The Bible records the lives of several men who willingly submitted to being held accountable—as well as others who avoided accountability. Let's take a look at two examples.

David was king of Israel, a man greatly used of God both in battle and composing many psalms of praise and worship. He desired to build a house for God, a Temple that would excel in beauty and permanence over the badger skin Tabernacle that had been in use for about four centuries. David shared his desire with the prophet Nathan, who encouraged David to begin the project, along with his blessing: "Then Nathan said to the king, 'Go, do all that is in your heart, for the LORD is with you'" (II Samuel 7:3). However, that night the Lord came to Nathan and told him to inform David he would not be the one to build the Temple; that honor would go to one of David's sons. David could have asserted his kingly authority and gone ahead with his plans, overriding the Lord's direction through Nathan. He even could have ordered that Nathan be imprisoned or even executed. Instead, he submitted to the word of the Lord through the prophet, and worshiped the Lord.

> For Your word's sake, and according to Your own heart, You have done all these great things, to make Your servant know them. Therefore You are great, O Lord GOD. For there is none like You, nor is there any God besides You. (II Samuel 7:21–22)

He submitted to the word of the Lord through Nathan and refrained from building the Temple. He began amassing materials his son would need to build the house of the Lord: a hundred thousand talents of gold, a million talents of silver, bronze and iron beyond measure, an abundance of iron for nails and cedar for timbers. (See I Chronicles 22.) He did all of this without resentment for being corrected.

Sometime later, a darker chapter in David's life unfolded when he committed adultery with Bathsheba and arranged for her husband Uriah to be killed in battle to cover up his evil deed. God sent Nathan to David to expose his sin by telling the story of a rich man having many sheep who took a poor man's only lamb and killed it instead of taking one of his own sheep. David became very angry and said the man who did such a thing should be put to death. Nathan looked straight into the eyes of King David and said, "Thou art the man!" Again, David's reaction was not one of anger or self-justification but one of humility and repentance. He submitted to the spiritual authority of the man God had placed in his life.

Contrast David's attitude with that of Solomon, the son who built the Temple. The Lord gifted Solomon with unparalleled wisdom and wealth, but over time he married many heathen wives and built temples for the idols his wives worshiped. Solomon at some time in his life must have studied the Torah, which contained warnings to kings such as "He [the king] must not take many wives, or his heart will be led astray" (Deuteronomy 17:17, NIV). However, I Kings 11:1–13 tells the story of Solomon's folly:

> King Solomon, however, loved many foreign women besides Pharaoh's daughter—Moabites, Ammonites, Edomites, Sidonians, and Hittites. They were from nations about which the LORD had told the Israelites, "You must not intermarry with them, because they will surely turn your hearts after their gods." Nevertheless, Solomon held fast to them in love. . . . As Solomon grew old, his wives turned his heart after other gods, and his heart was not fully devoted to the LORD his God, as the heart of David his father had been. (I Kings 11:1–2, 4, NIV)

Although Solomon could have sought counsel from Zadok the priest or Nathan the prophet, there is no record of him doing so; neither is there a record of any man of God speaking into Solomon's life about any of these things. After all, who can counsel the wisest man of all? Solomon was like a man traveling a winding mountain road in a whiteout with no guardrails or reflectors to help keep him safely on the road. So is every man who has no accountability in his life.

ACCOUNTABILITY IS A BIBLICAL PRINCIPLE

The heart is deceitful above all things, and desperately wicked: who can know it? I the LORD search the heart, I try the reins, even to give every man according to his ways, and according to the fruit of his doings. (Jeremiah 17:9–10)

Matthew 12:36–37 states, "But I say unto you, That every idle word that men shall speak, they shall give account thereof in the day of judgment. For by thy words thou shalt be justified, and by thy words thou shalt be condemned."

Romans 14:10–12 cautions us, "But why do you judge your brother? Or why do you show contempt for your brother? For we shall all stand before the judgment seat of Christ. For it is written: 'As I live, says the LORD, every knee shall bow to Me, and every tongue shall confess to God.' So then each of us shall give account of himself to God."

FELLOWSHIP VERSUS ACCOUNTABILITY

Most of our relationships never get past the surface level of conversation. We talk about the news, weather, sports, or some similar topic. If we ask someone, "How are you doing?" the answer most likely will be "Great" or "Not bad." Their kids may be failing in school or creating havoc in the home with their drama. Their wives aren't speaking to them and they are two months behind on their house payment, but they say, "Everything's fine. Just great!" The point is fellowship doesn't probe into the key areas of our lives because it has never been invited to do so.

WHY WE RESIST ACCOUNTABILITY

Accountability can be frightening because it requires us to be honest and transparent. We fear we might be rejected or thought of as weak and inadequate if someone were to really know what was going on in our life. The role models the world presents are the tough guys who can handle any problem, anywhere, without any help, that is not reality nor is it the description of a godly man.

Paul spoke of his own struggles with what he called a "thorn in the flesh." After he had prayed three times for the Lord to remove the thorn, this was the answer he received: "And He said to me, 'My grace is sufficient for you, for My strength is made perfect in weakness.' Therefore most gladly I will rather boast in my infirmities, that the power of Christ may rest upon me. Therefore I take pleasure in infirmities, in reproaches, in needs, in persecutions, in distresses, for Christ's sake. For when I am weak, then I am strong" (II Corinthians 12:9–10).

Now in case anyone might think Paul was a weakling, they need only read the following account in his ministerial résumé:

> From the Jews five times I received forty stripes minus one. Three times I was beaten with rods; once I was stoned; three times I was shipwrecked; a night and a day I have been in the deep; in journeys often, in perils of waters, in perils of robbers, in perils of my own countrymen, in perils of the Gentiles, in perils in the city, in perils in the wilderness, in perils in the sea, in perils among false brethren; in weariness and toil, in sleeplessness often, in hunger and thirst, in fastings often, in cold and nakedness—besides the other things, what comes upon me daily: my deep concern for all the churches. (II Corinthians 11:24–28)

I think you would have to agree he was one tough guy to endure all of that. Yet Paul confessed that his strength came from outside of his own abilities.

Paul held Peter and Barnabas accountable for their actions when they were in Antioch. Peter and the other Jewish Christians, contrary to kosher tradition, had been eating with the Gentile believers until a delegation of Jewish Christians came to town. Peter and Barnabas, fearing the criticism of the Jewish delegation, separated themselves from the Gentiles and ate only with the Jews. (See Galatians 2:11–14.)

Here was Peter, the apostle who had been given the keys to the Kingdom and had preached the first message on the Day of Pentecost, meekly taking correction for his actions. This is seen in a letter Peter would later write to those of "like precious faith": "And account that the longsuffering of our Lord is salvation; even as our beloved brother Paul also according to the wisdom given unto him hath written unto you." (II Peter 3:15).

As ministers, we must give an account of our stewardship and for those God has placed in our care. Hebrews 13:17 instructs, "Obey them that have the rule over you, and submit yourselves: for they watch for your souls, as they that must give account, that they may do it with joy, and not with grief: for that is unprofitable for you."

The writer of Hebrews addressed the responsibility of spiritual leaders who must give an account of those under their care. In turn, he admonished those under their leaders' authority to submit to their oversight and guidance because the leaders must give an accounting one day. Every child of God needs a shepherd (an overseer), not a dictator or overlord. They need someone who sincerely cares for their soul and offers encouragement, counsel, and correction as needed. Peter underscored this in his first epistle:

> Shepherd the flock of God which is among you, serving as overseers, not by compulsion but willingly, not for dishonest gain but eagerly; nor as being lords over those entrusted to you, but being examples to the flock; and when the Chief Shepherd appears, you will receive the crown of glory that does not fade away. (I Peter 5:2–4)

Peter went on to say in the following verse, "Likewise you younger people, submit yourselves to your elders. Yes, all of you be submissive to one another, and be clothed with humility, for 'God resists the proud, but gives grace to the humble'" (I Peter

5:5). Submission and accountability apply to everyone regardless of their office or position.

THE PROBLEM OF PRIDE

As ministers, we often struggle with pride. It is unrealistic—even insane—to think we always have to be right no matter what, that we can never admit our mistakes or shortcomings for fear we will get knocked off our pedestal—the pedestal we ourselves have built or one others may have placed us on. We must recognize and submit to the accountability the Lord has placed in the church for our benefit.

Paul, speaking to those who might think, "I'm in charge, so I must be right," said, "Let him who thinks he stands take heed lest he fall." (I Corinthians 10:12).

THE PROBLEM OF PERSONAL VULNERABILITY

When it comes to friendship, personal vulnerability is completely voluntary; but in an accountable relationship, personal vulnerability must be mandatory. To be vulnerable means to risk the disapproval of our accountability partner. No one wants to reveal their flaws and weaknesses to anyone. Accountability is an intentional decision that realizes the benefit is greater than the risk.

Accountability is an intentional decision that realizes the benefit is greater than the risk.

THE PROBLEM OF STRUCTURE

One reason men get into trouble is not because they don't know what they should do but because they have no structure in place. There is no one to hold them accountable and encourage them to do what is right.

The missing link is often accountability. We should regularly be answerable for each of the key areas in our life to a qualified person we have given permission to probe into our *moral, spiritual, relational, and financial lives;* in other words, "The Big Four". Proverbs 27:17 says, "Iron sharpeneth iron; so a man sharpeneth the countenance of his friend." We may have many acquaintances but still have few real friends who love and care for us enough to tell us what we need to hear, not just what we want to hear.

When Rehoboam ascended to the throne after his father Solomon, the people came and asked if he would relieve them of the heavy tax burden they had borne under Solomon. The elders told the young ruler, "If you will show kindness to the people and consider their request, they will serve you as they served your father." Unfortunately, Rehoboam's peers told him, "You should show them who's in charge and that you're going to be even harder and more demanding than your father Solomon!" As a result, Rehoboam found out the people "voted with their feet": ten tribes deserted the arrogant new king. Rehoboam's mistake was he took counsel with his out-of-touch peers who had grown up in the privileges of the palace and had no more experience or knowledge than he had. The young king, heady with newly acquired power and authority, rejected the wise counsel of the elders and brought about a tragic rebellion and division in the nation (I Kings 12:1–19).

Be careful whose counsel and guidance you submit to. Your peers may have the same blind spots you have. Hopefully, you still have your pastor and mentor in your life. Avoid chasing after prominent ministers and asking them to be your pastor. Paul wrote, "Though you have ten thousand instructors in Christ, yet you do not have many fathers..." (ICorinthians 4:15) The individual you give permission to hold you accountable should be someone you have the utmost confidence in; one whose counsel you are willing to submit to, and be totally honest with.

The real test of submission comes when you may not agree with the counsel you have received because it is not what you want to hear. You will fail the test if you only submit to the authority you agree with.

THE PROBLEM OF SUCCESS

How could success possibly be a problem? The danger is pride. Feeling you have arrived. You can now take advantage of your position and all of your hard work and effort. You may have others now who can help shoulder the load you have carried. Beware of becoming lax in your prayer life, coasting along on past deposits, Bible studies, and messages. There is nothing wrong with using materials you have used before, but make sure it is something fresh from the Lord for the congregation and not just a canned sermon.

Avoid the folly of Solomon, the wisest man on earth, who had no one to call him into account for his errors and disobedience to God's Word. No accomplishment or position you obtain will exempt you from the dangers and snares of sin. Keep your guard up.

Second Samuel 11:1 records at the time kings went out to battle, David remained in the comfort of his palace and sent Joab to lead the battle. We know the rest of the story. David saw Bathsheba and went on to commit adultery, then had her husband killed to cover up his sin.

It is not wrong to take a rest or enjoy a vacation. You and your family need it from time to time. However, you must never feel like you can take a vacation from your walk with God. Satan never takes a day off and he is looking for an opening to destroy you and everything God has done for you or allowed you to have.

Don't forget everything you have and where you are is because of God's goodness and mercy to you. (Refer to chapter 2, "Take Heed to Yourself.") This is one more reason for having accountability safeguards in place.

THE PROBLEM OF UNWILLINGNESS

The trouble with unwillingness is that it involves failure to admit there is a problem or even a potential problem. We must be willing to face our own vulnerability to sin and self-deceit. An addict who keeps telling himself he can handle his addiction without any help will remain under the power of his addiction. Likewise, a man who insists he needs no accountability over his life is courting disaster.

The real test of submission comes when you may not agree with the counsel you have received because it is not what you want to hear or do.

The following questions are offered to provide some guidance and structure to this matter of accountability. You should consider having a trusted mentor hold you accountable in these areas. You can use these same questions for those you are mentoring as well.

MAKE TIME EACH WEEK FOR THESE QUESTIONS

---

1. How has God blessed you this week? What went right?

2. What problem or concern has consumed your thoughts this week? What went wrong?

3. What has God shown you from His Word this week? Beware of the Bible becoming only a source for sermons.

Questions pertaining to spiritual life:

a. Describe your prayer life (for yourself, others, praise, confession, gratitude)

b. How is your relationship with Christ changing?

c. How have you been tempted this week? In what ways? How did you respond?

d. Do you have any unconfessed sin in your life?

e. Are you walking in the Spirit? What spiritual encounters have you had?

Questions Pertaining to Home Life

a. How is your relationship with your wife? Do you make time (date night or lunch) to talk with her and encourage the sharing of her feelings and concerns without letting the church dominate every conversation?

b. Do you let her know (words, gifts, helps, etc.) she is still the most special person in your life?

c. How is your relationship with your children? Are you spending quality time with them according to their ages and needs? Are you fun to live with? Are you intentionally teaching them values, discipline, and character? How effective are you in their spiritual training?

d. How are your finances? (e.g., stewardship, management, goals, give some, save some, spend some.) This often is an area of struggle for a young family and church-planter.

Questions Pertaining to Work Life

    a. How are things on your job: relationships, temptations, progress, stress, problems?

    Critical Concerns

    a. Do you feel in the center of God's will? Do you sense His peace?

    b. What are you wrestling with in your thought life?

    c. What have you done for someone else this week?

    d. Are your priorities in the right order?

    e. Is your moral and ethical behavior what it should be?

    f. How are you doing in your personal high-risk area?

    g. Are the "visible you" and "the real you" consistent in this relationship?

Keep the list close by and ask yourself how you are doing in these areas. You may not cover every topic each time you meet with your accountability partner, for there may be some area that needs additional time and attention. The main thing is someone has permission to ask you these tough questions and then motivate you to keep your guard up in these critical areas. This not an easy task by any means as the demands of family, church, and job are often very heavy. How much more reason do we have to seek God's grace and strength? The prayers and encouragement of those who, like ourselves, are trying to fulfill the call of God are vitally important!

God has equipped you to overcome the pitfalls and snares we have discussed. We are not to be ignorant of the devil's devices. Even more, we must know and appropriate the power, promises, and safeguards God has given to those He has called into His service. This is all intended to help you *follow the call* and finish well.

Chapter Nine

PASSING THE MANTLE

So he departed thence, and found Elisha the son of Shaphat, who was plowing with twelve yoke of oxen before him, and he with the twelfth: and Elijah passed by him, and cast his mantle upon him. (I Kings 19:19)

After an illustrious ministry as the prophet to the ten tribes of Israel, Elijah was instructed by God to anoint Elisha to take his place as the next prophet. He found young Elisha plowing a field with twelve yoke of oxen. Elijah trudged across the field, pulled his mantle from his shoulders, and without saying a word draped it over the shoulders of Elisha. Elisha knew the man of God and recognized the significance of the weight the elder prophet had placed on his shoulders. He ran after the prophet, saying, "Please let me say goodbye to my father and mother, then I will come with you." Elisha bade his family farewell, then followed the elder prophet and ministered unto him. The two prophets became devoted to each other over the next several years, until the day came when Elijah would be taken away by the Lord.

The sun was rising on the day they arrived at Gilgal, and its rays highlighted a pile of stones. These were the stones that had been taken from the middle of the Jordan River so many years before as a testimony of God's faithfulness in bringing Israel to the Promised Land. Elijah said, "Wait here, Elisha. I'm going to Bethel, where the Lord has sent me." Elijah refused to stay behind. They trekked westward thirteen miles to Bethel, the sacred place where their father Jacob had seen a vision of angels ascending and descending a ladder reaching into the heavens. The sons of the prophets asked Elisha, "Do you know your master is to be taken from you today?" Elisha replied, "Yes, I know. But don't speak of it."

After only a short rest, the elder prophet said, "Wait here, Elisha. I'm going to Jericho, where the Lord has sent me." Once again, Elijah refused to be left behind. If this truly was the day his beloved mentor was to be taken from him, he was determined not to miss it. They headed toward Jericho, almost twelve miles to the east, not far from where their journey had begun that morning. The sons of the prophets said to Elisha, "Do you know the Lord is going to take your master away today?" Elisha repeated, "Yes, I know. But don't talk about it."

After another brief stop, they continued about six more miles until they reached the banks of the Jordan River. Through the lengthening shadows Elisha saw a group of about fifty prophets who held back, watching them from a safe distance. Elijah pulled his shaggy mantle from around his shoulders, rolled it up, and struck the waters of the Jordan River. The waters separated, and they both crossed over on dry ground.

Elijah asked Elisha, "Tell me, what can I do for you before I am taken from you?" Elisha replied, "Let me inherit a double portion of your spirit." Elijah said, "You've asked a difficult thing, but nevertheless, if you see me when I'm taken from you, it will be yours." (See II Kings 2:9–10, NIV.)

They would have continued on their journey but were suddenly interrupted by a roaring whirlwind. Through the fading light burst a flaming chariot pulled by horses of fire, and Elijah was caught up into heaven.

Elisha cried out, "My father! My father!" and tore his garment in grief. His mentor had been taken away from him. He had served the elder prophet faithfully, witnessing the miracles and listening to his counsel, now that spiritual guide and example, that tower of strength, was gone. What would he do now that he was left on his own? Then Elisha heard a noise and looked up to see his master's old mantle floating down out of the heavens. The same mantle which had been placed around the young prophet's shoulders the day of his calling, now lay at his feet.

Second Kings 2:13 records, "He also took up the mantle of Elijah that had fallen from him, and went back and stood by the bank of the Jordan. Then he took the mantle . . . and struck the water, and said, 'Where is the LORD God of Elijah?'" The water divided, and he crossed over Jordan again, assured the God who had anointed and directed Elijah was with him as well. The mantle—the burden, the responsibility, the authority—of the old prophet had now passed on to him.

It has been said that "there is no success without a successor." We see this carried out as Joshua ministered to Moses, then completed the plan of God by leading the Israelites into their Promised Land. However, the narrative took an unfortunate turn for the worse at the death of Joshua. The book of Judges records the chaotic and sinful state of the nation because they lacked a clear line of succession following Joshua. Certainly, a succession of judges came forward during the three-hundred-year time span and delivered the people from their enemies, but when each judge passed off the scene without a successor, the people drifted away from God again.

There is no success without a successor.

Paul mentored Timothy and Titus to carry on the work he had begun and instructed them to teach and train others who would in turn continue on with the work of the Lord.

> *You therefore, my son, be strong in the grace that is in Christ Jesus. And the things that you have heard from me among many witnesses, commit these to faithful men who will be able to teach others also. (II Timothy 2:1–2)*

I recommend every minister regularly read Paul's pastoral letters to these young men. It will keep their focus on the duties and priorities set before them and may help avoid some pitfalls along the way.

All of us in the ministry today are part of a succession of apostolic ministers—those who have gone before us and those who will follow after us. In a relay race the most critical moment is the handoff of the baton as it is placed in the hand of the next runner. The ministry is similar, as the handoff or passing of the mantle is entrusted into the hands and care of the next generation of ministers and leaders.

We all stand on the shoulders of those who have paved the way before us, defending the faith and living through more difficult times than most of us face today. It is good to remember one day we too will pass off the scene and someone else will step into our place and ministry. This is the work of God. It is His church, purchased with His blood, and called by His name. We are simply called to be servants of the Lord and of His people during our allotted time.

When we start out in the ministry, we often are trying to do as much as we can for the Lord all by ourselves. True, sometimes there is no one else who can help share the load of ministry. However, as we grow older our emphasis should be on developing the next generation of ministers and leaders whom we hope will surpass us. Every Paul needs a Timothy and Titus to mentor. In turn, every young man needs a Paul in his life. This passing of the mantle ensures that legacy and ministry will continue in each succeeding generation.

This is an important principle to understand. Unfortunately, some men feel threatened by younger men rather than seeing them as assets and extensions of their own ministry and they fear empowering them.

There may be cause for concern, for they have witnessed some young men, who were more ambitious than righteous, eager to take charge, displacing and dishonoring the elder minister as being too old and irrelevant. These young men may have been talented, but their tarnished characters goaded them into causing a rebellion, perhaps driving out the elder, and splitting the church rather than waiting on God to open the doors for them.

The life of King Saul illustrates a leader filled with fear and jealousy because he felt threatened by David. Absalom, on the other hand, typified the actions of an ambitious, self-serving young man who felt his father David should be removed at all cost. God protected David from both of these threats and brought judgment on the transgressors. Eugene Peterson wrote an excellent book titled "The Tale of Three Kings," which covers these very things in greater detail. I highly recommend it.

In His perfect timing, God will both keep you and get you to the place He has prepared for you. You need not fear being replaced nor should you take matters into your own hands by grasping for position or manipulating people and circumstances for your own ambition. No one but you can prevent you from fulfilling God's plan and purpose for your life. Remember,

The steps of a good man are ordered by the LORD, and he delights in his way. (Psalm 37:23)

Much more could be written about the subject of mentoring, but the focus of this chapter is mainly directed toward younger ministers starting out to answer the call of God. While some may be called to plant a church feeling burdened for an unchurched area, many other young men will step into a pulpit and congregation someone else has founded or pastored before them. This transition needs some consideration and understanding to make it as smooth as possible for everyone involved: the congregation, the outgoing pastor, and the incoming pastor.

Ideally, the incoming pastor will have spent time in some area of ministry in the church and with the older pastor perhaps as an assistant or youth pastor. This allows time for everyone to know each other and understand the many aspects of a church family as well as its traditions and history. In other cases the out going pastor has relocated to another church and is no longer around.

Every situation is different when it comes to a church changing pastors. Some transitions are carried out in a smooth and orderly fashion that gives everyone time to adjust. Other transitions may come rather suddenly, as in the case of illness or death, creating an unexpected vacancy. Unfortunately, some churches have suffered scandal or moral failure and are left without a pastor. Other pastors might be retiring without any successor in place, so they or a church board may be responsible for finding a new pastor for the congregation. As you can see, there can be many variables in this process.

That is why every young minister needs his own pastor or elder he can trust to help guide him regarding situations he should avoid and which ones he should pursue. Of course, one must seek the will of God through much prayer and counsel before stepping into the role and responsibility of being a pastor and under shepherd.

Under the best of circumstances change can be difficult and requires getting used to. When you step into the role of pastor following a man who has spent many years caring for a congregation, it will take time for you to win their affection and loyalty.

The following is some advice stemming from my own years of experience and observation. It is not the final authority by any means. I'm offering this with the desire to be helpful and give you something to consider when the time comes for you to accept the call to pastor a congregation.

Give honor to whom honor is due. Don't be afraid to give honor and credit for the years of sacrifice and investment your predecessor has invested in the congregation before you arrived. If you are stepping into a new congregation that you have not previously been a part of, remember someone invested a great deal of time, love and sacrifice long before you arrived. Acknowledge that contribution when and where it is appropriate. In time, you too will have a lot invested there.

Give honor to whom honor is due.

I recommend in most cases that a retiring pastor put some time and space between himself and the church he has pastored for so long. Go on a well-deserved vacation and visit your family and friends. Enjoy this new season and give the new man an opportunity to become established.

In the case of a long-time assistant becoming the pastor and there is a good working relationship and understanding, the older minister may not need to relocate but become an honored elder/bishop.

If the transfer of leadership has been done correctly and the outgoing pastor has made it clear to the congregation, he is no longer the pastor to deal with their problems and issues but he is there now in agreement with the new pastor to help and support him. Then there should be no major issues. It may still be difficult for some of the people to make the transition as they are accustomed to calling on him and his wife for help. It will take time for them to get used to the change. Be patient; in time the people will regard you in the same way as they do their former pastor.

For a congregation, undergoing a change of pastors is much like a family changing parents; it can be traumatic for some. Undoubtedly, there will be things you would like to implement and change to fit your style and taste, but don't be in too big of a hurry. You are making a long-term commitment, so you don't have to overhaul everything right away. There is a sense of security in the familiar and routine, particularly in the areas of taste and preference (i.e., things that are not critical elements of doctrine or salvation). This is why a wise pastor will not try to change everything and everyone overnight just to suit his or his wife's style of music, décor, or order of the service. Hasty changes will only cause turmoil and may make the first few months or years unnecessarily more difficult.

The passing of the mantle is not easy to articulate, as there are no hard-and-fast rules. As stated above, every situation is unique. Of course, if the building is in need of repair and everyone knows it, then by all means get everyone together and set a course of action to fund and remodel as needed. Just be mindful not to run up a debt that will later become too burdensome to pay.

I came into a troubled church that had gone through a split. Many of the people were hurting and weren't ready to go out and save the world just yet. They needed time to heal and to learn to trust again. Fortunately, it was not my first pastorate. After many years in Asia as a missionary I had learned a little about patience. I spent the first year helping them get past the trauma, and in the process got to know the people one on one. I asked about their background, what they had been through, what their concerns were, and what their vision was for the future. I shared my story and vision with them as well. These simple acts proved to be of great benefit when we were ready to launch a building project a few years later.

I recommend every incoming pastor to a new congregation take time and get to know the people regardless of how good or how bad the situation may be. You can cast your vision from the pulpit, but you will be more effective in influencing them to follow you because of the time you spend getting to know each one personally.

If the church is small or relatively new, it usually doesn't take as long for people to adjust and get behind the pastor's vision. If it is an older congregation and its members are old enough to be your parents and grandparents, it might take longer to implement change.

Find out who put that old picture on the wall before you take it down. Don't be too quick to replace the Sunday school teacher or board member who has been there for thirty years through thick and thin. It may need to be done, but you would do well to learn the art of solving problems and saving relationships.

---

*Learn to solve problems and
save relationships if at all possible.*

Try to put yourself in the other person's place and imagine how you would feel and respond to the ideas and changes you want to introduce. Sometimes it is best to offer suggestions and ideas, then give people time to process them. You may have already reached a conclusion because you have been thinking it over for some time. You have weighed out all the options, while others may not have given any thought to it yet.

After leaving Egypt, Joshua and Caleb could have made it to the Promised Land in a matter of weeks, but if they wanted to take anyone with them, it would take much longer. You want to take as many folks along with you as you can, so be patient. Take your time when making or introducing any major changes.

Keep in mind the man who will follow you someday may wonder what took you so long to get to where you are.

You are called to feed and lead His sheep. Some are young and eager to move on, while others are older and more cautious. All deserve to be loved, respected, and cared for by their pastor. Sheep need and respond to a shepherd, not a high-powered CEO driving them.

This transition of passing the mantle will take place in every minister's lifetime, perhaps more than once. It requires understanding one's place of service in the kingdom of God and His timing for each one. It requires great respect and appreciation on the part of both men. For the young man who will step into the position the older minister has held, treat him with the love and respect you would want shown to you. To the older minister stepping aside, remember when you started out you had much to learn but you made it with the help of God. Through your prayers and support the young man following you will make a successful transition. Together you carry on the legacy of passing the mantle.

Chapter Ten

FINISHING WELL

I have fought a good fight, I have finished my course, I have kept the faith: henceforth there is laid up for me a crown of righteousness, which the Lord, the righteous judge, shall give me at that day: and not to me only, but unto all them also that love his appearing. (II Timothy 4:7–8)

These words of the apostle Paul should encourage every minister. Paul didn't minimize the effort required to accomplish and fulfill his call, but he kept his focus on the reason and reward behind all the effort. There is a crown of righteousness, a reward for faithfulness, given to all those who love and long for the appearing of the Lord.

Solomon wrote, "Better is the end of a thing than the beginning thereof" (Ecclesiastes 7:8). Solomon's observation is the completion and accomplishment of a task is better than the anticipation or beginning of it.

Every parent has great dreams and expectations for their children, but only time will reveal if they live up to and fulfill their potential. The same can be said for those who answer the call of God to enter the ministry. Only time will reveal their true character, commitment, and accomplishments.

The word picture Paul paints for us regarding his own life and ministry depicts a struggle against opposition. He said he had fought a good fight: he was alert and stayed aware of all things; he was instant in season and out of season; he endured afflictions; he did the work of an evangelist; he made full proof of his ministry. He wrote, "I have finished my course." This depicts an image of a grueling endurance race, not just a short sprint to the finish line. Paul wrote in I Corinthians 9:24–27 (ESV):

> Do you not know that in a race all the runners run, but only one receives the prize? So run that you may obtain it. Every athlete exercises self-control in all things. They do it to receive a perishable wreath, but we an imperishable. So I do not run aimlessly; I do not box as one beating the air. But I discipline my body and keep it under control, lest after preaching to others I myself should be disqualified.

Last, Paul said he had kept the faith—the doctrine that had been delivered to him. His faith in God had stood the test. Let's examine the word picture he has given us.

I HAVE FOUGHT A GOOD FIGHT

If we are to finish well, we too must continue to fight the good fight of faith, for difficult times come to all in this battle. You will face spiritual opposition to the work of God. You will have struggles with people—conflicts and misunderstandings.

At times you will struggle with your own heart and mind as you are called to surrender your will and agenda to God and trust in His. Paul referenced this battle in Ephesians 6:12: "We do not wrestle against flesh and blood, but against principalities, against powers, against the rulers of the darkness of this age, against spiritual hosts of wickedness in the heavenly places." These unseen spiritual forces are very real, and they work against us and what God is wanting to do through us.

Again, in II Corinthians 10:4–5, the apostle used the imagery of effort and struggle:

> *For the weapons of our warfare are not carnal, but mighty through God to the pulling down of strong holds;) casting down imaginations, and every high thing that exalteth itself against the knowledge of God, and bringing into captivity every thought to the obedience of Christ.*

We are promised victory, but it does not come without a struggle nor does it come with human effort alone. *Spiritual needs always require spiritual resources.*

Yes, there are struggles we will all face at times but there are also great victories we are promised and can be assured of! "Behold I give unto you power (*authority*). . . over all the power (*ability*) of the enemy and nothing shall by any means hurt you" (Luke 10:19). You can be confident if God brings you to it, He will bring you through it! This is a spiritual life and battle, requiring spiritual resources to accomplish it. You have available everything you need to win it.

I recall the story of a boy who came home after school with his shirt torn and a black eye. He told his mother, "That was a good fight!" Is mother looked at him and asked, "What was so good about it?" With a big grin the boy looked up and said, "I won!" What makes this fight worthwhile is we have read the back of the book…. and, "We win!"

I HAVE FINISHED MY COURSE

We may finish different seasons and ministries God has appointed to us along the way but we are never truly finished as long as we still have breath. Retirement may seem lightyears away from you right now as you are launching into ministry. Even then, there is no place to sit down and do nothing as long as you have the health and strength to serve. The harvest field is still ripe and plenteous.

My brother-in-law and his wife, Everett and Lois Corcoran, spent almost thirty years as missionaries to Pakistan and Asia. When they returned to their home in New Brunswick, Canada, they reopened several churches that had been without a pastor and continued to be active until his health failed and he went on to be with the Lord at the age of eighty-seven. We are never truly finished with our course until the Lord calls us home.

Everyone will find their course is unique in many ways, for it is the path the Lord has chosen for them personally to follow. Not all are called to serve overseas, or travel as an evangelist, or plant a church, but whatever calling God places upon you or wherever He calls you to serve, it is your course to run and to finish without getting distracted by what others may or may not be doing. Keep in mind this is His church, His kingdom, and His agenda; we are called simply to fulfill His will. A lifetime is made up of days, so live each day for the Lord and for His glory and you too will finish the course He has set before you.

I HAVE KEPT THE FAITH

Throughout his good fight and the course, he ran until the finish line, Paul kept the faith. He kept it in trying circumstances, among false brethren and unjust treatment. Truly, it is your faith in God, your faith in His Word, and your faith in the whole body of Christian doctrine that is under fire and spiritual attack. It involves staying true to the apostolic doctrine, "once delivered to the saints" (Jude 1:3) even though others may have discarded it as no longer relevant in our modern culture. Paul warned of this in 2 Timothy 4:1-7

"I charge you therefore before God and the Lord Jesus Christ, who will judge the living and the dead at His appearing and His kingdom: 2 **Preach the word!** Be ready in season and out of season. Convince, rebuke, exhort, with all longsuffering and teaching. 3 For the time will come when they will not endure sound doctrine, but according to their own desires, because they have itching ears, they will heap up for themselves teachers; 4 and they will turn their ears away from the truth, and be turned aside to fables. 5 But you be watchful in all things, endure afflictions, do the work of an evangelist, **fulfill your ministry.**" (emphasis added)

Keeping our own faith is also part of the struggle. You must wait on the promises and hold on to your faith when everything around you speaks of failure and defeat, when you see little or no results from your efforts and the enemy mockingly asks, "Where is your God?"

Seldom do things move as quickly as we would hope. There are setbacks along the way, and at times we may seem to be up against a wall. I'm reminded of the words God spoke to Joshua before the battle of Jericho began: "See! I have given Jericho into your hand, its king and the mighty men of valor" (Joshua 6:2). Joshua was staring at the huge walls, knowing that behind them the enemy were all armed and ready for battle. Before it ever happened, the Lord said, "See, I have given this city and all the men in it to you already." Our God still sees and calls things that are not, as though they already were accomplished. He has promised you His presence and provision. See! Not with your natural eyes but with your spiritual eyes through His Word. Your faith must be anchored in God's Word, and praying in the Spirit. That is how to keep the faith.

THERE IS A CROWN

Paul revealed why he regarded all this effort as being worthwhile: "Henceforth there is laid up for me a crown of righteousness, which the Lord, the righteous judge, shall give me at that day: and not to me only, but unto all them also that love his appearing" (II Timothy 4:8). He was keeping his eye on the goal and reward the Lord he loved and served would give him one day.

The goal is to faithfully follow the call of God and serve Him wherever He has placed you. The following was covered earlier but let me mention it once again. Success is not going to be measured by comparing your work with someone else's. It will not be measured by how large your building is or how many attend your services each week. It will be measured by God's priorities. A love for God; a servant's heart and being faithful through the long haul. Like a couple standing at an altar exchanging their wedding vows to love and cherish each other through the good times and the bad, until death alone shall cause them to part. It is easy to say "I do," but it will take a lifetime commitment to fulfill it.

Like every minister, you will face many distractions and discouragements as you press toward the finish line in this race. The course that has been set before you may not always be clear and smooth. It is critical to keep your eye on the goal as the following story illustrates.

Florence Chadwick loved to swim and accomplished many long-distance swimming feats. She was the first woman to swim across the English Channel both ways; she even swam across the Strait of Gibraltar. On July 4, 1952, she set out to swim twenty-one miles across the Catalina Channel from Catalina Island to Palos Verde on the California Coast. The weather was challenging that day, and the water was ice cold. The fog was so thick she could barely see the support boats following her. The tide and currents were against her and there were sharks in the area. She set out anyway, hoping the fog would lift. Hour after hour she swam, but the fog never lifted. After about fifteen hours she began to doubt her ability to finish the swim. Unable to see the coastline, she asked her team to lift her out of the water. She was less than a mile from the coast when she gave up. Later she said, "If I could have seen the land, I know I could have made it." Two months later she tried it again. Although the fog was just as dense this time, she pressed on and made it in record time—thirteen hours and forty-seven minutes.

Obstacles are what you see when you take your eyes off the goal.

While there may be many short-term goals involving ministry—whether it be a church plant, a call to the mission field, or even completing a building project; the ultimate and most important goal is to serve the Lord and be found acceptable in His sight. It is then you will hear Him say, "Well done, thou good and faithful servant."

God has equipped you with everything you need to succeed and accomplish His plan and purpose for your life. There is a process in life and learning every minister will go through as he or she grows, matures, and is conformed into His image and likeness. But remember, "What shall we then say to these things? If God be for us, who can be against us?" Romans 8:31

The few chapters and thoughts covered in *Following the Call* are by no means all that could be said regarding the ministry. My sincere desire and motivation for writing this book has been to touch on a few areas that might help young ministers navigate through some of the challenges that will come and avoid the pitfalls that have caused some to become casualties.

I hope you have enjoyed this time together as much as I have in sharing this with you.

Finally, my friend, keep yourself in the love of God. Keep your heart with all diligence. Hide His Word in your heart. Pray without ceasing. Be accountable. Love your spouse and family. Keep your eye on the goal, as you are *Following the Call* and you too will finish well!

Made in the USA
Coppell, TX
21 November 2020

41855940R00080